X

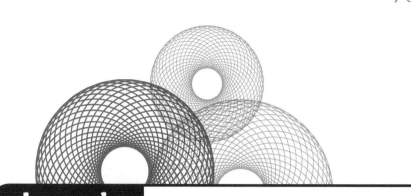

teen's guides

LIVING
with
DEPRESSION

D0166584

AUG 26 2009

Also in the
Teen's Guides series

Living with Anxiety Disorders
Living with Asthma
Living with Cancer
Living with Diabetes

teen's guides

LIVING
with
DEPRESSION

Allen R. Miller, Ph.D.

☑️Checkmark Books®
An imprint of Infobase Publishing

Teen's Guides
Living with Depression

Checkmark Books
An imprint of Infobase Publishing, Inc.
132 West 31st Street
New York NY 10001

Library of Congress Cataloging-in-Publication Data

Miller, Allen R.
   Living with depression / Allen R. Miller.
      p. cm. — (Teen's guides)
   Includes index.
   ISBN-13: 978-0-8160-6345-1 (hardcover)
   ISBN-10: 0-8160-6345-1 (hardcover)
   ISBN-13: 978-0-8160-7562-1 (pbk.)
   ISBN-10: 0-8160-7562-X (pbk.) 1. Depression in adolescence. I. Title.
   RJ506.D4M548 2007
   618.92'8527—dc22   2007000554

Checkmark books are available at special discounts when purchased in bulk quantities for businesses, associations, institutions, or sales promotions. Please call our Special Sales Department in New York at (212) 967-8800 or (800) 322-8755.

You can find Facts On File on the World Wide Web at http://www.factsonfile.com

Text design by Annie O'Donnell
Cover design by Jooyoung An

Printed in the United States of America

Sheridan FOF 10 9 8 7 6 5 4 3 2 1

This book is printed on acid-free paper.

CONTENTS

What Is Depression?

"I felt as if a curtain dropped one day and I fell into the deepest, darkest abyss. That's what I've been battling for more than four years. My depression interfered with every conceivable part of my life."

—Marla, 17

Susan is a bright, talented 19-year-old who has struggled with feelings of overwhelming sadness for most of her teenage life. "I can't remember when I wasn't depressed," she says. Although doctors believe her sad feelings probably began in childhood, she didn't realize there was anything wrong until she went away to college. "I tried Rolfing, transactional analysis, and meditation," she recalls. "I cut out coffee, smoking, and alcohol. I went on vegetarian diets, juice diets, and fasts. I kept trying all these alternative therapies because I thought that something should help the way I felt."

Eventually, Susan was referred to a psychiatrist, who prescribed antidepressants and cognitive-behavioral therapy for what he told her was one of the worst cases of depression he said he'd ever seen. Susan says her whole world has changed. "I feel great," she says. "I feel *normal.*"

Perhaps you felt like Susan sometimes. Or maybe your mom or dad, brother or sister, grandparents—or friends—seem to be depressed a lot. You probably know someone who's depressed, because this problem affects as many as one of every 33 children and one of every eight teens of every color, race, economic status, or age.

More conservative estimates suggest that major depression affects 1 percent of all preschoolers, 2 to 3 percent of elementary school–aged children, and 6 to 8 percent of teens. Yet as many as two-thirds of kids with depression don't get the help they need, according to the National Mental Health Association. Not surprisingly, kids who have a learning disorder or attention problem are also at high risk for developing depression. Although boys and girls have the same risk of developing depression during early to middle childhood, the risk among girls rises much higher as puberty begins; teen girls are twice as likely as boys to be depressed.

BIOLOGY AND THE BRAIN

Most experts would agree that major depressive disorder is caused by a combination of brain chemistry, family history, distorted thinking, and emotional environment. While it's not certain which of these factors is the most important, abnormal levels of certain brain chemicals are known to be closely linked with depression. Therefore, the cause of depression is often attributed to a chemical imbalance.

Every minute of the day, your brain is processing complex thoughts and emotions. It does this by producing and breaking down various chemicals, including hormones and neurotransmitters (chemical messengers that influence mood and emotions). The way your body produces, breaks down, and absorbs these neurotransmitters inside and outside nerve cells plays an important role in how you experience pleasure and moods. The chemicals also may make you more vulnerable to depression.

For a long time scientists have been investigating the possibility that mood problems may be linked to the level of neurotransmitters (called norepinephrine, serotonin, and dopamine) in the brain. One of the strongest arguments in favor of the idea that neurotransmitters and depression are linked is that drugs that improve depression directly affect these neurotransmitters. For example, tests show that many depressed people have low levels of the neurotransmitter serotonin. When such people take an antidepressant that affects these levels, the serotonin between cells rises. The result is that the depressed person taking this drug often feels better. (Some research has found that cognitive-behavioral therapy also affects parts of the brain related to mood—although different parts from that targeted by medications.)

But serotonin is just one type of neurotransmitter. Evidence suggests that many kinds of neurotransmitters may influence depression and mood in unknown ways. More and more, scientists are realizing that neurotransmitters act in the brain in incredibly complex ways, interacting like a neural symphony to affect emotions, thoughts, and other processes throughout the entire body.

In fact, the brain is so complex that scientists believe neurotransmitters may not be the only chemicals in the brain that affect mood. Hormones, too, seem to play a role. Whereas each neurotransmitter acts at a very specific spot in the brain (the space between nerve cells), hormones travel through the blood, carrying messages to groups of cells or organs all over the body. Hormones play a vital role in managing the body's stress responses, so they may be involved in the development of depression as well. For example, when you're under stress, levels of a hormone called cortisol rise. This so-called stress hormone fluctuates from one moment to the next, depending on how much stress you feel. Stress can be physical (you just ran a marathon) or emotional (you just broke up with your boyfriend), but either way, the cortisol levels in your body rise. You might be upset, but you would also feel more alert and ready to take action.

In a healthy person, cortisol levels drop when the stress passes. Unfortunately, in some people, this cortisol control mechanism doesn't work well, and cortisol levels remain high whether the person is stressed or not. This can lead to a variety of problems, including high blood pressure, and may make you more vulnerable to depression.

CAN YOU INHERIT DEPRESSION?

It seemed to Jim that both his parents had always struggled with depression. He remembers being told that his mother had been hospitalized with severe depression after he was born. His dad's alcoholism seemed to be triggered by feelings of bleakness. By the time Jim was in high school, he, too, was diagnosed with depression and given a prescription for antidepressants.

Sometimes Jim thought his family must be cursed. Why were they all so miserable, all the time? Did he learn how to be depressed just from growing up in a depressed household? Or had he inherited the tendency to feel the way he did?

Scientists believe that there are, in fact, some types of depression that run in families. A person has a 27 percent chance of inheriting depression from one parent—and more than a 50 percent chance if both parents are affected. Twin studies show that there's a 70 percent chance for both identical twins to suffer from depression—twice the rate at which depression co-occurs in fraternal twins.

If depression runs in your family, you could inherit a biological vulnerability—a tendency—to develop depression yourself. Genes supply the instructions for how the brain develops and for everything it does. But there are many competing instructions; for example, a variety of chemicals carry messages inside and between cells. This complicated circuitry groups into major pathways with specific jobs, such as regulating mood or storing memories. Your genetic makeup is important because genes influence the way these pathways function—and that can trigger depression.

Humans can inherit many tendencies or traits. For example, if your mom is shy, you could inherit the behavioral trait of shyness, too. The good news is that if you do inherit a behavioral trait or a tendency to a problem such as depression, you can do something about it.

Moreover, not everyone with the genes for a vulnerability to depression will develop the illness. Scientists believe that other factors, such as stress at home, work, or school, are also involved—and a nurturing environment and positive support can provide some protection.

OTHER CAUSES OF DEPRESSION

In some families like Jim's, major depression crops up in generation after generation. But depression also can occur when there is no family history of depression at all. It usually takes a combination of genetic, psychological, and environmental factors to trigger a depressive disorder.

While it doesn't seem as if depression strikes certain personality types more than others, it does seem that your temperament and how you think of yourself and others could make you more vulnerable. Kids with low self-esteem, who tend to think of themselves and the world with pessimism (the glass is always half empty), or who are readily overwhelmed by stress can be prone to depression. So can kids who seem to have trouble accepting their good points, or those who have a bad temper. Whether these symptoms represent a psychological tendency to develop depression—or an early form of depression—is not clear.

Illness. In recent years, researchers have discovered that physical changes in the body can be accompanied by mental changes as well. Medical illnesses such as stroke, heart attack, diabetes, cancer, and hormonal disorders (such as hypothyroidism) can cause depressive illness, making the sick person apathetic and unwilling to take care of physical needs, thus prolonging the recovery period. Clinical depression should not be considered a normal reaction to such illness.

Stress. As mentioned above, stress affects the hormone levels in your body and can lead to depression. All kinds of stress can contribute to the development of depression: In some people, a severe depressive episode can be triggered by a serious loss, issues in a relationship, financial problems, or even a good grade on a test. Depression is also more common in people with a history of trauma, sexual abuse, physical abuse, physical disability, alcoholism, and troubled families. Later episodes of depression typically can then be precipitated by only mild stresses or none at all.

In particular, stress after the loss of loved ones, such as the death of close family members or friends, can trigger depression in vulnerable people. If you experience this kind of stress and you've inherited certain genes that make you more vulnerable to depression, you may be at higher risk of developing depressive illness. Stressful life events may trigger a new episode of depression in some people, while others experience recurrent depression for no apparent reason at all. Scientists also believe that social isolation or early-life deprivation may lead to permanent changes in brain function that can make a person more vulnerable to developing depression.

Age. Many people experience their first bout of depression during adolescence, although they may not realize it. Typically, the onset of depression occurs most often between ages 15 and 19; some research suggests as many as 20 percent of high school students are deeply unhappy. This may not be news to you—after all, being a teenager isn't always a picnic. Sometimes it can feel as if nothing is going right, and you may feel burdened with stress from your parents' expectations and your struggles to do well in school, to make and keep friends, to have a boyfriend or girlfriend, to look attractive or be successful in sports. These factors put teenagers at higher risk for depression.

Gender. Whether you're a boy or a girl also can affect your risk of developing depression. Major depressive disorder affects twice as many girls and women as boys and men. It could be that hormones raise a girl's vulnerability. One recent study discovered that depressive mood swings and physical symptoms of premenstrual syndrome (PMS), which affects up to 7 percent of menstruating girls and women, are caused by an abnormal response to normal hormone changes during the menstrual cycle. Some experts also believe that the higher rate of depression in girls and women also could be related to the roles they learn in society.

A girl's hormones help regulate her response to stress, and this hormonal circuit is overactive in many people who are depressed. The hypothalamus pumps out a substance called corticotropin releasing factor (CRF) when a girl's brain detects a threat. Higher levels of CRF trigger hormone secretion by the pituitary and adrenal glands to prepare her to fight or run away. Some research suggests that if her hormonal system gets stuck in "overdrive" and constantly pours out hormones, she may develop depression. Depressed people have extra-high CRF levels that drop when they take antidepressant drugs; as the hormone levels drop, their depression improves.

Diet. A lack of certain vitamins, such as folic acid and B_{12}, may cause depression. Low levels of these vitamins also can interfere with the way that antidepressant medication works.

Drugs That May Cause Depression

Accutane (acne drug)

benzodiazepines (CNS depressants)

birth control pills

clonidine (high blood pressure drug)

cortisone-like steroids

digitalis (heart drug)

indomethacin (anti-inflammatory drug)

levodopa (Parkinson's disease drug)

methyldopa (blood pressure drug)

phenothiazines (antipsychotics)

reserpine (blood pressure drug)

Substance abuse. Experts know that depression can lead people to drink too much alcohol or abuse drugs to make themselves feel better. Today, scientists also suspect that substance abuse can cause depression.

Medications. Some medications that people use for a long period of time may cause depression. Some of these drugs may include certain blood pressure medicines, sleeping pills, and even birth control pills in some cases.

Other links between certain drugs and depression are not so clear. For example, some patients have become depressed or developed other serious mental problems while taking the acne medicine Accutane or soon after stopping Accutane. Critics argue that severe acne itself can cause depression and suicidal thoughts, and that it has nothing to do with a medication designed to treat it. The U.S. Food and Drug Administration (FDA) continues to assess reports of suicide or suicidal thoughts associated with Accutane. The FDA warns that anyone who takes this medication should be closely observed for symptoms of depression or suicidal thoughts. If the patient becomes irritable or anxious, has other symptoms of depression, or has thoughts of suicide, a health care professional should be contacted right away.

WHAT YOU NEED TO KNOW

➤ Depression affects between 6 and 8 percent of teens, yet as many as two-thirds of kids with depression don't get the help they need.

➤ Children and teens with learning disorders or attention problems are at high risk for developing depression.

➤ Teen girls are twice as likely as boys to be depressed.

➤ Most experts agree that major depressive disorder is caused by a combination of brain chemistry, family history, and emotional environment. Stress, diet, medications, substance abuse, and physical illness also can play a part.

➤ Your temperament and how you think of yourself and others could make you more vulnerable to developing depression.

➤ Onset of depression occurs most often between ages 15 and 19.

2

What Is Bipolar Disorder (Manic Depression)?

For most of her life—beginning in her preteens—Caitlin drifted along in a depressive fog that blunted her feelings and actions, making her feel listless and unproductive. But it wasn't until she graduated from college, when an antidepressant sent her into a manic state, that bipolar disorder was correctly diagnosed. Her older brother had been diagnosed with bipolar disorder several years before, but her own disease had been mild enough to elude identification for years.

Bipolar disorder is a serious disorder of the brain often confused with depression alone. It causes severe swings in mood, energy, thinking, and behavior. Although bipolar disorder—once known as manic depression—affects about 2 million adult Americans, according to government estimates, experts aren't sure how many children and teens have the condition. In fact, much remains unknown about how this disease affects kids, and it can often be tough to diagnose in younger people.

What scientists do know is that there are four types of bipolar disorder: bipolar I, bipolar II, cyclothymic disorder, and bipolar disorder–NOS (not otherwise specified). Symptoms of bipolar disorder are different in different people, so experts have come up with these four groups to better classify symptoms. Knowing what type of bipolar disorder a person has makes it easier to tailor treatment to specific symptoms.

Bipolar I. This form causes alternating episodes of intense mania and depression.

Bipolar II. This type of bipolar disorder causes episodes of mild mania that occur between recurrent periods of depression. Symptoms of this milder mania can include a markedly excited or irritable mood, along with increased physical and mental energy. Many successful people have experienced great creativity during periods of mild mania.

Symptoms of Bipolar Disorder

It's a good idea to consult a mental health professional if four or more of these symptoms occur for more than two weeks at a time:

Typical Manic Symptoms

> ▸ racing speech and thoughts

> ▸ lots of energy

> ▸ less need to sleep

> ▸ exaggerated optimism

> ▸ "daredevil" behavior

> ▸ feelings of self-importance

> ▸ inappropriate or early sexual experiences

> ▸ extreme irritability and explosive anger

> ▸ aggressive behavior

> ▸ extreme happiness or silliness

> ▸ talking too much, too fast; changing subjects too quickly; refusal to be interrupted

> ▸ delusions

> ▸ impatience

> ▸ poor judgment

Cyclothymia. Kids and teens with this form of the disorder experience periods of less severe but still pronounced mood swings.

Bipolar disorder–NOS (not otherwise specified). This diagnosis is used to describe a person's condition when it isn't obvious what type of bipolar disorder the person has. For this diagnosis, there is no typical pattern, and it may not be clear if the person has fully developed symptoms of type I or II.

- ➤ reckless behavior (spending too much, making rash decisions, driving wildly)

- ➤ concentration problems or unusual distractibility

- ➤ substance abuse

Typical Depressed Symptoms

- ➤ loss of interest in favorite activities

- ➤ prolonged sad mood

- ➤ fatigue or lack of energy

- ➤ feelings of guilt or worthlessness

- ➤ sleeping too much or too little

- ➤ drop in grades

- ➤ concentration problems

- ➤ inability to take pleasure in things once enjoyed

- ➤ eating too much or too little

- ➤ suicidal thoughts

- ➤ frequent complaints of illnesses such as headaches or stomachaches

SYMPTOMS

Bipolar disorder influences the way the brain works, which in turn affects the way a person thinks, feels, and acts. A person with bipolar disorder typically has persistent episodes of mania (feeling "high" or excited) interspersed with continuing periods of deep depression. Sometimes a person might have mixed state, in which some symptoms of mania and depression occur at the same time.

Of course, everyone feels excited or sad sometimes—that's completely normal. But the shifting moods of a person with bipolar disorder are far more intense. A person with bipolar disorder may not just feel happy or excited; he or she may feel like the strongest or most powerful person on Earth. This can make the person do things he or she might not otherwise do, such as be less careful when driving, spend too much money, abuse alcohol or drugs, or take unusual risks. When the depression mode kicks in, the person with bipolar disorder may not just feel a little blue or sad but plummet into a deep, dark despair.

Bipolar disorder affects both boys and girls. While most people experience their first symptoms in their early 20s, more and more often the condition is appearing during the teenage years. Sometimes even young children can be diagnosed.

Kids vs. adults Unfortunately, bipolar disorder in childhood or adolescence usually causes different symptoms than in an adult. Kids with bipolar disorder may have much more rapid mood changes and may be more likely to be irritable or anxious, so that their mood disturbance is continuous—a mixture of mania and depression. This rapid and severe cycling means that there aren't very many periods of wellness between episodes. Adults typically experience an episode of mania or depression for weeks or months at a time. In contrast, kids with this condition are much more likely to be irritable, destructive, or violent instead of euphoric or elated.

Some kids and teens experience irregular, unpredictable symptoms, while others may always experience a manic episode in the same way, right after depression (or vice versa). Sometimes episodes follow the seasons; for example, a burst of mania in the summer may be followed by depression in the winter.

Between episodes, a person with bipolar disorder usually returns to normal functioning, but some people don't have this normal break. These people have constant symptoms that may change either very quickly or very slowly. Rapid cycling between mania and depression is much more common in women, children, and teens.

Some people with bipolar disorder abuse alcohol and drugs as a way of feeling better, but these substances can make symptoms worse.

Early-onset bipolar disorder. Some researchers also think that kids who develop symptoms in childhood or the early teenage years may have a more severe type of bipolar disorder than people who develop symptoms in later adolescence or adulthood. When the symptoms appear before or soon after puberty, they often tend to be a continuous, rapid-cycling, and irritable state that occurs along with disruptive behavior disorders (especially attention-deficit/hyperactivity disorder [ADHD]). People who develop the condition later in life tend to develop manic symptoms suddenly with more stable periods between episodes. ADHD also tends to occur less often when the disease develops later in life.

CAUSES

Scientists aren't sure what causes bipolar disorder, but most experts think that chemical, genetic, and environmental factors all may be involved.

Brain chemicals. The onset of bipolar disorder seems to be strongly related to the chemicals in the brain. Many experts believe bipolar disorder is caused by an imbalance in brain chemicals called neurotransmitters that normally affect mood.

Heredity. Genes also play a role in bipolar disorder. If a close family member has bipolar disorder, there's a higher risk that others in the family will also be afflicted. However, bipolar disorder can skip generations and take different forms in different individuals. Having someone with the condition in the family doesn't mean that you'll automatically inherit it. Even having an identical twin with the condition doesn't mean you'll have the same problem. But because there is a higher risk, researchers are trying to find the genes that help trigger bipolar disorder.

Environmental factors. Sometimes, bipolar disorder can be triggered by events in your life. For some kids, emotional stress such as their parents getting divorced, serious money problems, or a death

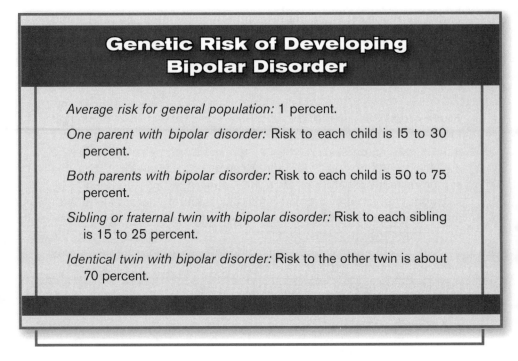

Genetic Risk of Developing Bipolar Disorder

Average risk for general population: 1 percent.

One parent with bipolar disorder: Risk to each child is l5 to 30 percent.

Both parents with bipolar disorder: Risk to each child is 50 to 75 percent.

Sibling or fraternal twin with bipolar disorder: Risk to each sibling is 15 to 25 percent.

Identical twin with bipolar disorder: Risk to the other twin is about 70 percent.

in the family can trigger the first episode of mania or depression. Sometimes just going through puberty can cause an episode. Girls may find that their symptoms are linked to their monthly menstrual cycle.

DIAGNOSIS

It's not easy to diagnose bipolar disorder—you can't just take a simple blood test to reveal the problem. There aren't any brain scans or X-rays that can identify the condition, yet without proper diagnosis and treatment, the disorder can become worse, leading to hospitalization, trouble with the law, drug abuse, or suicide.

Bipolar disorder is especially difficult to recognize in children and teens because it doesn't match the symptoms in adults and because the symptoms also resemble those of other common childhood disorders, such as schizophrenia, post-traumatic stress disorder, ADHD, and simple depression. Sometimes bipolar symptoms are mistaken for normal childhood emotions and behavior. Unlike these normal mood changes, however, bipolar disorder interferes a great deal with function in school, with friends, and at home.

According to several studies, many of the 3 million children and adolescents diagnosed with depression in the United States may actually have bipolar disorder but have not yet experienced the manic phase of the illness. Because children and teens with bipolar disorder don't usually have the same symptoms as adults with the condition, a mental health professional must examine a teen's behavior carefully before making a diagnosis. The doctor will write down a history of the person's experiences and may order a medical exam to rule out other conditions.

Once the illness appears, without treatment, episodes tend to recur and get worse. Early intervention and treatment can make an enormous difference.

TREATMENT

Typically, it takes about 10 years after symptoms first appear before treatment is begun. People with bipolar disorder can't just "snap out of it." Bipolar disorder isn't a character flaw or emotional weakness. It's not a condition that can be improved by simply wanting to get better, eating healthier food, or taking vitamins. It's a serious medical condition that requires treatment.

Medication. While there's no cure for bipolar disorder, a combination of medication and counseling can help even out a person's moods and control symptoms. A doctor will probably prescribe mood-stabilizing medication (most often lithium, valproate, or carbamazine) to reduce the number and severity of manic episodes and to help prevent depression. These medications may be balanced with carefully selected antidepressants. Other medications may be used to treat insomnia and agitation after a manic episode, such as the antianxiety medicines lorazepam (Ativan) and clonazepam (Klonopin), antipsychotic medicines such as risperidone (Risperdal), or an anticonvulsant, such as valproate (Depakote).

Correct diagnosis by conducting a thorough, thoughtful psychotherapeutic interview is the key to ensuring that the right medication is prescribed. A doctor who only identifies the depression and misses the manic state might prescribe antidepressants, and research suggests that using an antidepressant to treat depression in a person who actually has bipolar disorder may induce manic symptoms if the antidepressant is taken without a mood stabilizer (such as lithium). Moreover, a doctor who misdiagnoses a person with ADHD instead of bipolar disorder might prescribe stimulants, and using stimulant medications to treat ADHD-like symptoms in a child with bipolar disorder also may worsen manic symptoms.

Psychotherapy. A psychologist or other type of therapist will provide counseling to help the person better understand the condition, adapt to stress, rebuild self-esteem, and improve personal relationships. Psychotherapy can greatly reduce the stress that can trigger manic and depressive episodes. However, psychotherapy tends to be more helpful for people with depression than with mania, since individuals in a manic phase often have trouble concentrating and retaining new information.

Three types of psychotherapy are particularly useful for depression: behavioral therapy, cognitive therapy, and interpersonal therapy. Modern psychotherapy for depression is usually aimed at either changing your behavior (behavioral therapy) or changing both your thoughts and your behavior (cognitive-behavioral therapy). Cognitive therapy focuses on identifying and changing the thought distortions and beliefs that can lead to depression. Interpersonal therapy focuses on reducing the strain that a mood disorder can place on relationships.

Just like kids with other types of chronic medical conditions such as asthma or diabetes, children and teens with bipolar disorder need to work together with their doctors to find the best treatment. Typically, you would meet each week for about 12 weeks with a trained mental health professional (a psychiatrist, psychologist, social worker, or counselor) to learn how to deal with your depressive symptoms.

WHAT YOU CAN DO

There is a lot you can do to manage your own symptoms. You should try to read all you can about the condition and talk to your family about how you feel. You and your family might find it helpful to join a local support group for kids or family members with bipolar disorder.

It's also very important to take any medications just the way the doctor tells you to. Be sure to report any uncomfortable side effects right away, but don't change the medication or stop taking it abruptly without talking to your doctor.

Limiting stress and getting plenty of sleep are also important. Try to go to bed and get up at the same time every day. Irregular sleep patterns seem to be linked to chemical changes that can trigger mood episodes.

Anyone with bipolar disorder should avoid alcohol or drugs, because this can affect how the brain works, triggering symptoms and interfering with medications. You should even be careful about how much caffeine you use each day. (Caffeine is contained not just in coffee, but also in chocolate, tea, and some over-the-counter medications for colds, allergies, or pain.) Even small amounts of caffeine can interfere with sleep, your mood, or the medicine you take.

As you probably know, just dealing with the pressures of being a teenager can be hard—every adolescent normally faces problems with friends, school, and family. Adding bipolar disorder into the mix can make this period of life even tougher. But working together with your doctor and your family can help you learn how to cope with your symptoms and lead a much more normal life.

WHAT YOU NEED TO KNOW

> ‣ Bipolar disorder is a serious disorder of the brain that causes severe swings in mood, energy, thinking, and behavior.
> ‣ Although bipolar disorder affects about 2 million adult Americans, experts aren't sure how many teens have the condition.
> ‣ There are four types of bipolar disorder: bipolar I, bipolar II, cyclothymic disorder, and bipolar disorder–NOS (not otherwise specified).

> • Bipolar I causes alternating episodes of intense mania and depression.
> • Bipolar II causes episodes of mild mania between recurrent periods of depression.
> • Cyclothymia is a type of bipolar disorder that causes periods of less severe but still pronounced mood swings.
> • Bipolar disorder–NOS (not otherwise specified) describes a person's condition when it isn't obvious what type of bipolar disorder is emerging.

> ‣ Symptoms include persistent episodes of mania ("high") interspersed with continuing periods of depression; a mixed state includes symptoms of both mania and depression at the same time.
> ‣ Teens with bipolar disorder usually have different symptoms than adults, with more rapid mood changes, more irritability or anxiety, and a mixture of mania and depression.
> ‣ Symptoms appearing before or soon after puberty tend to involve a continuous, rapid-cycling, and irritable state that occurs along with disruptive behavior disorders (especially ADHD).

➤ Most experts believe that bipolar disorder is caused by chemical, genetic, and environmental factors.

➤ Diagnosing bipolar disorder requires a very careful mental health evaluation; early intervention can make an enormous difference, but untreated bipolar disorder tends to get worse over time.

➤ Bipolar disorder can't be cured, but a combination of medication and counseling can help even out a person's moods and control symptoms.

➤ Mood-stabilizing medication (most often lithium, valproate, or carbamazine) can reduce the number and severity of manic episodes and help prevent depression; antidepressants also may be prescribed.

➤ Counseling can help you better understand the condition, rebuild self-esteem, improve personal relationships, and reduce the stress that can trigger manic and depressive episodes.

➤ You can help yourself by learning about bipolar disorder, joining a local support group, taking medications correctly, limiting stress, getting plenty of sleep, maintaining regular patterns, and avoiding alcohol and drugs.

Is It "the Blues" or Depression?

Sara was 15 years old and just didn't think she could face another day at school. As she lay in bed, the thought of getting up and reaching for her favorite jeans seemed like just too much trouble. What was the point? She didn't have any friends at school. She felt like a loser, and she just knew everybody else was laughing at her behind her back. What was worse, she'd been feeling like this for almost a month, and she felt as if she couldn't take one more single day.

Feeling down? Having trouble shaking off the blues? You're not alone. Everyone gets sad and depressed—sometimes even hopeless. What's particularly hard for some teens to understand is that their peers are struggling with exactly the same sorts of insecurities and uncomfortable feelings. Many of even the best-looking class leaders who get top grades and seem so successful are struggling with everyday feelings of being down sometimes. And some of them are hiding much more serious depression under that successful facade.

THE BLUES V. DEPRESSION

Sadness and depression are pretty common—but there's a difference between a normal low feeling and a serious (doctors call it *clinical*) depression. Sadness is a normal human emotion that occurs when you feel like you've lost something important, or if you've been disappointed, or even if something bad has happened to someone you care about. And when you're lonely, you'll often feel sad. If your pet dies, you lose a school election, fail a test, your best friend is mad at you, or that special person doesn't want to go out with you—any of those things can make you feel sad, and that's perfectly normal.

Loss and separation are the most common causes of sadness, because it can be heartbreaking to lose someone or something you care about. More serious sadness—the particular kind of sadness you feel after a person or animal you love dies—is called grief. But loss isn't just about a death—other kinds of loss or separation involving people you care about (such as divorce) also can make you feel sad. You also might feel sad when you leave something or someone behind, such as when you move to a new house or leave your old school. Even getting a new sister or brother may make you feel sad, even if everyone else is excited and expects you to be thrilled about your new sibling. Usually, the feelings of sadness after a loss slowly get better as weeks and months pass, although for a really big loss you'll probably always feel a little bit sad.

While relationships with other people can make you happy most of the time, tension or fighting can cause sadness. Many kids fight more with parents and siblings as they get older and become more independent. You may fight about clothes, money, your hair or makeup, how you're doing in school, or your friends.

Teenage friendships can be fraught with difficulties as you struggle to find a place where you fit into the world. You might feel sad when things aren't going well between you and your friends and family or if you get yelled at. In school, worrying about your grades or tests may make you sad, too. Sometimes, kids who are sad might also feel angry or guilty. You might feel like blaming someone.

Some people have normal sad feelings just once in a while, but others may have sad feelings pretty often. More than half of teenagers and plenty of younger kids go through a sad period at least once a month. When you're sad, life may seem dark or even hopeless. It may seem as if there's nothing to look forward to. You may feel flat or empty. When you're in a sad mood, it may feel like it will last forever, but if you think about it clearly, those feelings of sadness don't last very long—a few hours, or maybe a day or two.

If sad feelings go on for too long, hurt too much, or make it hard for you to enjoy your life, it's called depression. That deeper, more intense kind of sadness that lasts a lot longer is diagnosed as a serious, clinical depression. That kind of unrelenting sadness that lasts for weeks or months is not normal, even if it was triggered by something bad.

MILD AND SEVERE DEPRESSION

Depression can occur in two forms—you can be mildly depressed (a condition doctors call *dysthymia*) or you can be severely depressed (called *major depression* or *major depressive disorder*), but fortunately both types can be successfully treated.

Mild depression. Parents and teachers often ignore dysthymia in children and teenagers because they assume the person is just a little sad and that these feelings will pass soon. What many people don't understand is that such a persistent low mood can lead to severe depression or substance abuse if it's not treated appropriately. Dysthymia is less severe but often more stubborn to treat than major depression; it can be diagnosed if you've felt depressed for at least a year and you also have at least two other symptoms of major depression. Many kids with untreated learning disorders also develop dysthymia. (These specific symptoms are discussed later in this chapter.)

Major depression. Major depression involves severe, intense symptoms of sad or low mood that last for weeks at a time. It's important to identify the difference between normal sadness and a serious depression, because 90 percent of kids who are depressed respond to treatment—but only if it's first recognized as a problem. All too often, that doesn't happen. While experts estimate that 5 percent of all teenagers are depressed, fewer than a quarter of those who are depressed ever get help. Unfortunately, too many times parents and other adults assume that feeling down, depressed, and bad about yourself is something to be expected during adolescence, and they tend to overlook all kinds of uncomfortable behavior.

Depression in children. Most children get sad or depressed once in a while if they get yelled at or their best friend plays with someone else on the playground. But these feelings pass in a day or so. If the sadness deepens or lingers beyond two weeks, it could indicate a more serious problem. Most people think that children can't get depressed, but that's not true—it can happen at any age, even to young babies.

Depressed children may seem unusually clingy or tired, listless or anxious. Some may start to lose interest in everyday activities and simply refuse to get up and go to school. Others may begin to try to hurt themselves. A child who is severely depressed may even try to commit suicide—even as young as age five or six.

While the average length of depression in a young child is about seven months, the younger the child, the more serious the outlook.

Depression in teens. Depression becomes even more common in teens between 15 and 19. Depressed teens usually have low self-esteem and are very self-critical; they may be uncooperative, over-sensitive, negative, restless, antisocial, or aggressive. But because these symptoms are to some degree what many consider typical teen behavior, a teens' true depression may be undiagnosed. That's what happened to Janet, who at 15 has struggled with depression for several years. Convinced that she was both overweight and unattractive, her behavior became increasingly outrageous and destructive until her teachers finally convinced her parents to seek counseling for their daughter.

Adjustment disorder with depressed mood. If a child or teen gets depressed after a stressful event, this pattern may be called a reactive depression, or adjustment disorder with depressed mood. This is especially likely if there has been a major disruption or change in the person's life and he or she is already struggling with another issue, such as a learning disability or ADHD. For example, if you have dyslexia and your family moves to another school district, this could trigger the onset of an adjustment disorder.

Are You at Risk for Depression?

Depression isn't particularly rare in children and teens, but some kids are at higher risk than others. Those who are at higher risk include kids who

- ▶ are under stress

- ▶ have experienced loss

- ▶ have attention, learning, or conduct disorders

- ▶ are girls

- ▶ have a family history of depression.

The symptoms of this type of depression are a lot like those of other depressive disorders, except they don't last as long. (Symptoms usually appear within three months of the stressful event and typically last no longer than three to six months.)

If you're having an adjustment disorder with depressed mood, you might feel sad, cry a lot, lose interest in normal activities, or not feel like being around other people. You might defy your parents or skip school, fight, or act reckless. Your grades may start to slide, and you might start fighting with your closest friends. Teenagers are especially liable to develop an adjustment disorder with depressed mood. They often get depressed in reaction to stress when they don't think there's a solution to their problem. In such cases, finding a reasonable solution to the stressful event is a key part of getting better.

EMOTIONAL SYMPTOMS OF DEPRESSION

While symptoms may differ from one child or teen to the next and may depend on the severity of the depression, the following emotional signs are typical of depression. If you or someone you know has at least four of these symptoms, you may want to consider professional help:

- *Feeling sad, worthless, hopeless, numb, helpless:* These feelings are with you most of the time, every day.
- *Feeling guilty:* These feelings may be exaggerated or inappropriate to the situation, so that you feel guilty for things that aren't really your fault, for minor mistakes, or for things that you really can't control.
- *Irritability or restlessness:* You might be short-tempered and find it hard to relax.
- *Loss of interest in former activities:* You may no longer care about hobbies or friends you used to enjoy.
- *Low energy*
- *Concentration problems*
- *Drop in grades or school performance*
- *Neglecting appearance*
- *Drug or alcohol abuse*
- *Trouble making decisions:* Depression can make it hard to think clearly or concentrate, so that even trying to make a simple choice can seem overwhelming.
- *Thoughts or talk of death or suicide:* You may feel so low that you have thoughts about killing yourself to stop the pain. Other kids may attempt to hurt themselves.

PHYSICAL SYMPTOMS

While you may be mostly aware of the emotional symptoms of depression, people who are depressed also can experience many kinds of physical problems that are caused by depression. For example, depression can slow down your digestion, which can cause stomach problems, and it can affect how you feel pain as a result of changes in the same chemicals that cause depression. Many experts think that depression can make you feel pain differently than other people.

Some of the physical symptoms that can indicate depression include:

> *Appetite change:* Some people with depression lose their appetite, while others find themselves craving certain foods (especially carbohydrates and sweets). This can lead to significant weight loss or gain.

> *Back pain:* People who already have back problems can experience a worsening of symptoms if they become depressed.

> *Fatigue:* Many depressed people feel exhausted all the time, no matter how much they sleep. Getting out of the bed in the morning may seem impossible.

> *Stomach or intestinal problems:* If you're depressed, you also might feel queasy or nauseated or have diarrhea or constipation.

> *Headaches:* It's not unusual for people who are depressed also to have headaches. If you already suffer from migraines, they may get worse if you're depressed.

> *Muscle and joint pain:* Depression can make any kind of chronic pain worse.

> *Sleep problems:* Whether it's sleeping too little or much more than normal, both problems have been linked to depression.

CONSEQUENCES: THE RISK OF SUICIDE

One of the reasons to be concerned about kids who are depressed is that if the condition is untreated, it can lead to suicidal thoughts and even suicidal acts. In the past 25 years, while the numbers of suicide have generally decreased, the rate of suicide for young people aged 15 to 24 has tripled. In fact, most experts rate suicide as the second or third most common cause of death among kids aged 10 to 14. While no one is sure exactly why so many teens are thinking about suicide or even taking their own lives, depression is known to be one of the biggest reasons.

When all hope seems lost, some kids and teens feel that suicide is the only solution. It isn't. In fact, research has shown that almost everyone who commits suicide has a mental disorder such as depression or a substance abuse problem, according to the National Institute of Mental Health. This means that the feelings that often lead to suicide are highly treatable—if the problem is identified in time.

Warning signs. The challenge, of course, is to figure out whether a person is depressed enough to be thinking about suicide. This is very important: You must consider any talk about wanting to die or commit suicide to be a real risk. Severe alcohol or drug abuse is also

Suicide Warning Signs

There is no typical suicide profile, but the following signs may suggest that the person is thinking about an attempt. Professional help should be sought immediately if you recognize yourself, a friend, or a family member in this list.

- ▶ Threats of suicide: it is not true that people who threaten won't follow through
- ▶ Life crisis: death of loved one, parental divorce, trouble at school
- ▶ Behavior change: altered attitude or energy level
- ▶ Appearance change
- ▶ Aggression: sudden interest in dangerous pursuits or unsafe sexual practices
- ▶ Mood change: for example, sudden calmness
- ▶ Gift-giving: sudden distribution of favorite items to friends or family
- ▶ Withdrawal: unwillingness to communicate, desire to be alone, withdrawing "into a shell"
- ▶ Poor school performance: sudden drop in school performance or grades signaling a withdrawal

a major warning sign, because that's one of the first things troubled teens try to do to make themselves feel better.

If a teen has tried to commit suicide before, there's a higher chance he or she will try again. Boys who have made attempts in the past are at particularly high risk for repeat tries. Also, many kids or teens who have committed suicide have a family history of suicide (this could be linked to either heredity or imitation). A severe stress, such as trouble with the police, fighting at school, or breaking up with a girlfriend or boyfriend, also may trigger a suicide attempt. There is also a direct link between the availability of guns at home and the risk for suicide. The more guns there are, the easier they are to get, and the higher the risk. Accounts of suicide in the news also can trigger suicide in a vulnerable teen.

The best thing to do if you are suicidal, or you suspect someone else is suicidal, is to try to talk about these feelings.

WHAT YOU NEED TO KNOW

▶ There's a difference between a normal low feeling and a serious (doctors call it *clinical*) depression.

▶ Depression can occur in two forms—mild (*dysthymia*) or severe (*major depression* or *major depressive disorder*).

▶ Depression after a stressful event is called reactive depression or adjustment disorder with depressed mood.

▶ Depression is diagnosed if there are at least four of the following symptoms: constant sadness, worthlessness, hopelessness, numbness, helplessness, guilt, irritability or restlessness, loss of interest in former activities, low energy, concentration problems, drop in grades or school performance, neglecting appearance, substance abuse, trouble making decisions, thoughts or talk of death or suicide.

▶ Physical symptoms of depression include appetite change, back pain, fatigue, gastrointestinal problems, headaches, muscle and joint pain, and sleep problems.

▶ Untreated depression can lead to suicidal thoughts and acts; any talk about wanting to die or commit suicide is a real risk.

4

Getting a Diagnosis:
Where to Turn

Debbie was an introspective, sensitive teenager who struggled in school with an undiagnosed reading disability and a nagging feeling of unhappiness. "For so many years, life has seemed so gray," she finally told her mother during her first year of college. "Everything seems like a gray fog. I can't think, and I can't concentrate."

For almost as long as she could remember, she said, she struggled against that "gray fog" that cloaked her life with unhappiness. It wasn't until she read about the symptoms of depression in a psychology textbook that she realized the examples sounded like her. She asked her mother for a referral to a psychologist, who promptly diagnosed clinical depression and recommended a combination of therapy and medication. After a few months of family and individual psychotherapy and a brief course of antidepressants, Debbie was overjoyed to realize that the gray fog had faded away.

"She's like a different person," her mother reports. "She's stopped arguing all the time, and she seems much happier. She's also doing better in school, and she even likes to read!"

If you've been struggling with depressed or sad feelings like Debbie was, you may have been wondering if there is something wrong. If your problems are persistent and interfere with the way you want to live your life, you need to check with a health care professional to find out if your moods are a symptom of something more serious.

But if you're like many people, you may not be sure how to get help or where to go to get the best care. Some kids feel comfortable talking about their sad feelings to their parents, but other kids may not. There are many other adults you can talk to, such as teachers, doctors, school counselors, or grandparents. You may want to ask your friends who *they* feel safe talking to about their feelings. Or the next time you visit your pediatrician, you might see if you can broach the topic with the doctor or a nurse. Perhaps you feel closer to your religious (pastoral) counselor—these spiritual experts are also trained in mental health issues and may be able to help you find a good mental health counselor.

The important thing is to talk to someone you trust about your feelings—someone who can give you some guidance about what to do next. Find someone whom you can trust, who's easy to talk to, and who will listen to your feelings. Remember, you're not weird and you're certainly not the only person who's ever felt this way. There's someone who will understand and be willing to help you. If the person you confide in thinks that you might really have a problem with depression, ask if he or she can recommend a good psychologist, psychiatrist, social worker, or pastoral counselor.

FIRST STOP: YOUR FAMILY DOCTOR

If you've been feeling depressed, it's usually a good idea to check with your pediatrician or family doctor first. This way, you can make sure you don't have a physical illness that might be causing symptoms, before consulting a mental health professional. The doctor will

Government Referrals on the Internet

The government offers a Mental Health Services Locator at

http://www.mentalhealth.samhsa.gov/databases

This Web site provides information about mental health services and resources in each state. You can access this information by clicking on your state to reveal a list of helpful resources and referrals.

In an emergency . . .

If you're in a crisis, the emergency room doctor at your local hospital can offer temporary help right now and can refer you to a mental health expert for further treatment.

perform a complete physical exam and may order tests to make sure you're completely healthy. If your doctor can't find any physical reason for your depression, he or she may be able to make a referral to a mental health specialist for further evaluation. Most doctors have working relationships with mental health specialists and can probably recommend someone you'll like.

FINDING A MENTAL HEALTH EXPERT ON YOUR OWN

If you prefer not to involve your doctor or anyone at school, you can look for a mental health expert on your own or ask your parents to look. You can ask friends, colleagues, or family members for referrals. If you live near a university, the department of psychiatry or psychology may offer private or sliding scale–fee clinic treatment options.

You also can check the yellow pages under "mental health," "health," "social services," "suicide prevention," "crisis intervention services," "hotlines," "hospitals," or "physicians" for phone numbers and addresses. Call your local medical or mental health societies for referrals, or check with a state or national professional society such as the American Psychiatric Association, the American Psychological Association, the National Association of Social Workers, or the American Association of Pastoral Counselors. Experts in cognitive-behavioral therapy can be found on the Web sites of the Academy of Cognitive Therapy (academyofct.org) and the Association for Behavioral and Cognitive Therapies (abct. org). These Web sites can give you a list of names of members near you.

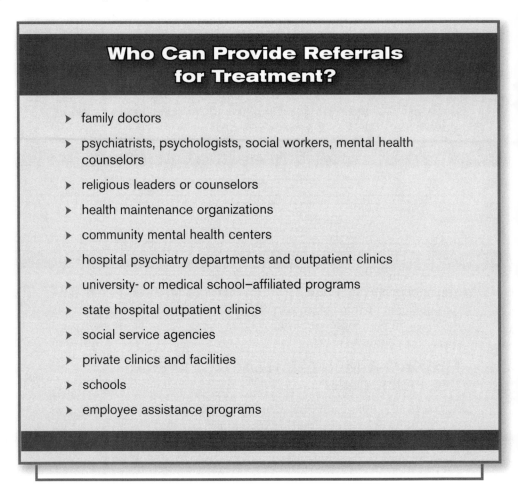

Who Can Provide Referrals for Treatment?

- ▶ family doctors
- ▶ psychiatrists, psychologists, social workers, mental health counselors
- ▶ religious leaders or counselors
- ▶ health maintenance organizations
- ▶ community mental health centers
- ▶ hospital psychiatry departments and outpatient clinics
- ▶ university- or medical school–affiliated programs
- ▶ state hospital outpatient clinics
- ▶ social service agencies
- ▶ private clinics and facilities
- ▶ schools
- ▶ employee assistance programs

WHAT KIND OF SPECIALIST?

A referral may involve any number of specialists trained to treat depressive disorders. Just like other health professionals, mental health therapists may hold a variety of credentials and specific degrees. As a general rule, your therapist should have a professional degree in the field of mental health (psychology, social work, or psychiatry) and be licensed by your state. Psychologists, social workers, and psychiatrists all diagnose and treat mental health disorders.

Beyond their degrees, there are a number of differences among psychologists, psychiatrists, social workers, and pastoral counselors. If you do have a depressive disorder, it's best to get treatment from a professional who has been trained in the type of treatment that works best for these problems—a kind of psychotherapy called cognitive-behavioral therapy or behavioral therapy (described in Chapter 5). Since medication also may be used to help treat depressive disorders, your psychologist, social worker, or counselor will probably work closely with a psychiatrist or other physician who can prescribe medications when they are required. (If you live in New Mexico or Louisiana, specially trained psychologists licensed in that state can prescribe medication.)

The following is a general breakdown of the different experts who can help you deal with your depression.

Psychologist (PhD, PsyD, or EdD). This type of mental health expert specializes in the diagnosis and treatment of mental or emotional problems; many specialize in treating children and teens and their families. Clinical psychologists often use a range of tests to assess, diagnose, and treat patients. A psychologist usually holds a doctoral degree from a university or professional school, requiring four or more years of graduate school and a year of supervised internship. Most states also require an additional year of supervised experience for a psychologist to earn a professional license in this area. (In only a few states, professionals with a master's degree in psychology can be licensed as psychologists.) A psychologist in clinical practice usually has a degree in clinical psychology (although it could be in counseling psychology, school psychology, or educational psychology).

A psychologist has studied emotions and behavior processes and uses this knowledge to help teens understand and change their behavior. Many psychologists have received special training, such as in family psychotherapy, depressive disorders, or neuropsychology. Because psychology is such a broad field, it's important for you to find out if the psychologist you're considering has good training and experience in the particular kinds of problems with which you're struggling.

Psychiatrist (MD or DO). A psychiatrist is a medical doctor who specializes in the diagnosis and treatment of disorders of thinking, feeling, and behavior. They can prescribe medication and therefore often work with psychologists in prescribing antidepressants or other drug treatments.

Psychiatrists must complete four years of medical school and at least three years of residency training in medicine, neurology, and general psychiatry. After completing medical school, graduates must pass a licensing test given by the board of medical examiners for the state in which they want to work. Those who want to work with children also must be board certified in child and adolescent psychiatry, requiring extra years of training. Psychiatrists must be recertified every 10 years.

Social worker (LCSW). A licensed clinical social worker provides mental health services to prevent, diagnose, and treat mental, behavioral, and emotional disorders. Clinical social workers must have a master's or doctorate degree in social work, with an emphasis on clinical experience. They must undergo a supervised clinical field internship. They may be licensed by their state after successfully passing an exam and meeting all requirements. All states have licensing, certification, or registration requirements regarding social work practice and the use of professional titles.

An LICSW is also a licensed clinical social worker; a CSW is a certified social worker. Many social workers are trained in psychotherapy, but you should know that credentialing requirements vary from state to state. Likewise, the meaning of designations (i.e., LCSW, LICSW, CSW) may vary from state to state as well.

Social workers with a master's degree in social work (MSW) may be eligible for the Academy of Certified Social Workers (ACSW), the qualified clinical social worker (QCSW), or the diplomate in clinical social work (DCSW) credential based on their professional experience.

Pastoral counselors. A pastoral counselor is trained in both psychology and theology. Teens might meet with a pastoral counselor to address their depression in the context of religion and spirituality. In general, the fees of pastoral counselors are lower than those of other health care professionals; counseling by a certified pastoral counselor is generally covered by health care plans if the pastoral counselor is a licensed professional counselor by the state. However, remember that pastoral counselors are not medical doctors and cannot prescribe medication. While some pastoral counselors are licensed by the state, most states do not require it because of the clergy exemption clause. However, laws vary significantly from state to state.

CHOOSING THE BEST EXPERT
As you look for someone to help treat your depression, don't be afraid to spend some time checking out different experts before you make a decision. The two of you will be working as a team to discover the exact nature of your emotional problems. Together, you'll be

Handy Initial Decoder

There are a variety of credentials for mental health professionals. Here's what they mean:

AAMFT American Association for Marriage and Family Therapy (cert)*

AAPH American Association of Professional Hypnotherapists (cert)

ABFamP American Board of Family Psychology (cert)

ABMP American Board of Medical Psychotherapy (cert)

ABPH American Board of Psychological Hypnosis

ACT Academy of Cognitive Therapy (cert)

ACP advanced clinical practitioner (lic)**

ACSW Academy of Clinical Social Workers (cert)

BCCS board certified in clinical social work (cert)

BCDSW board certified diplomate in clinical social work (cert)

CCCP board certified in child and adolescent psychology (cert)

CCMHC certified clinical mental health counselor (cert)

CCSW certified clinical social worker (lic)

CISW certified independent social worker (cert)

CMFT certified marriage and family therapist (cert)

CP certified psychologist (lic); clinical psychologist (lic)

CSW certified social worker (lic); clinical social worker (lic)

D/AABM diplomate, American Academy of Behavioral Medicine (cert)

D/ABPN diplomate, American Board of Psychiatry and Neurology

DSW doctor of social work

EdD doctor of education

(continues)

(continued)

LCP	licensed clinical psychologist (lic); licensed counseling professional (lic)
LCSW	licensed clinical social worker (lic)
LGSW	licensed graduate social worker (lic)
LICSW	licensed independent clinical social worker (lic)
LMFC	licensed marriage and family counselor (lic)
LMFCC	licensed marriage, family and child counselor (lic)
LMFT	licensed marriage and family therapist (lic)
LMHC	licensed mental health counselor (lic)
LP	licensed psychologist (lic)
LPA	licensed psychological associate (lic)
LPC	licensed professional counselor (lic)
LSP	licensed school psychologist (lic)
LSW	licensed social worker (lic)
MC	master of counseling
MFC	marriage and family counselor (lic)
MFCC	marriage, family and child counselor (lic)
MFCT	marriage, family and child therapist (lic)
MSS	master of social science
MSSW	master of science in social work (acad)
MSW	master of social work
NAMHC	National Academy of Mental Health Counselors (cert)
NBCC	National Board of Certified Counselors (cert)
NCC	National Certified Counselor (cert)
NRHSPP	National Register of Health Services Providers in Psychology (cert)
PhD	doctor of philosophy

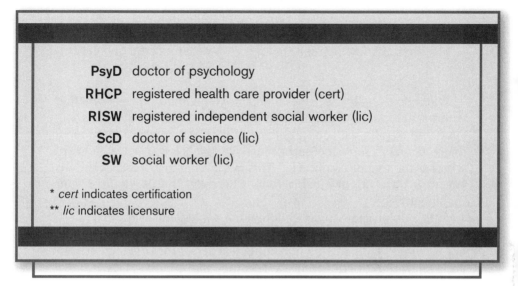

PsyD doctor of psychology
RHCP registered health care provider (cert)
RISW registered independent social worker (lic)
ScD doctor of science (lic)
SW social worker (lic)

* *cert* indicates certification
** *lic* indicates licensure

developing a plan to treat your disorder that may involve medication, cognitive-behavioral or other talk therapy, or a combination of methods. That's why it's so important that you feel comfortable working with the therapist and asking questions about the process.

While the therapist's experience and education is important, you must find a counselor with whom you feel comfortable, because you'll be sharing some very personal thoughts and feelings with this person. It's also important that you feel comfortable with whatever therapy the mental health professional suggests. The more you trust this person and feel comfortable in exploring your feelings, the better.

Let's say a family friend has recommended a mental health specialist who is dedicated to treating depression in teens. When your parents talk to this person on the phone to discuss payment options and insurance issues, there are a few other things they should find out.

1. Your parents should ask if the therapist is licensed to practice in your state, what type of experience he or she has, and whether he or she has been trained in cognitive-behavioral or interpersonal psychotherapy.
2. Your parents also should find out if the person primarily has worked with children and adolescents.
3. It's a good idea for your parents to ask the therapist to meet with you for a brief consultation or talk with you during a

phone interview before you commit to becoming a client. Your parents should expect to pay for this type of service, although a few therapists might consider it a complimentary visit.

When you finally meet the therapist, you should find out whether you're comfortable with the person. How well does the therapist help you understand what your problems may be and what your treatment might involve? You'll be surprised how quickly you get a sense of whether the two of you "click." This is the time to ask any questions you may have. It's not being rude—the right "fit" is vital for your treatment.

At this point, many older children and adolescents want to be reassured that anything they say to the therapist is confidential and cannot be shared with anyone (including teachers, other doctors, or your parents) without permission—unless they indicate that they may try to hurt someone or commit suicide. This is very important to discuss with the therapist right away, but you'd be surprised how often kids hesitate to bring this up. Even worse, some kids simply shut down and don't tell the therapist what's really going on in their lives out of fear that the counselor will tell their parents.

That's what happened to Phoebe, who had been depressed for several years when she suddenly confided to a friend that she'd started cutting herself and that she was frightened by her own behavior. "But I can't tell my therapist," she confided, "because I'm afraid he'll tell my parents." Luckily for Phoebe, a teacher saw the scars and intervened. It would have been much better if Phoebe had discussed with her therapist right at the beginning of treatment how private their sessions would be.

Most therapists like to give parents a general sense of what's going on in therapy, but if there are important things you want to talk about in complete privacy with the therapist, most will keep your confidence. Most therapists are very sensitive about the importance of finding a balance between a parent's legitimate right to know what's going on with a child and the child's innate right to privacy.

Some examples of other questions you might want to ask a potential therapist include

☐ What kind of treatment will you recommend?
☐ If I need medication, can you prescribe it or refer me to someone who can?
☐ How long might treatment take?
☐ How often will we need to meet?

☐ Are you available by phone if I have an emergency? Who will I see when you're sick or on vacation?

☐ Will you also meet with my parents if that would help?

Pay attention to how the person answers these questions and how he or she responds. If you decide that the person seems ideal and really sensitive to you, that's wonderful. But if something just doesn't feel right, don't worry about moving on and continuing the search.

WHAT TO EXPECT DURING THE DIAGNOSTIC SESSION

During this first appointment, you won't be examined like you would be at your physician's office, and there aren't any needles. You'll just sit in a comfortable chair and talk. Your mother or father might come in with you. Younger children might play games or sometimes draw pictures with the therapist. The mental health expert will try to get to know you better. If one of your parents comes, too, the three of you might talk together about your depression and how long your sad feelings have been bothering you.

Diagnosing depression in teens can be tricky because early symptoms are sometimes hard to pinpoint. The most important way that a mental health expert can tell if you are clinically depressed is to combine careful interviewing with a detailed review of your behavior. An expert also may use one of the following questionnaires to screen for the depressive disorders, which include major depressive disorder (unipolar depression), dysthymic disorder (mild depression), and bipolar disorder (manic depression):

➤ Children's Depression Inventory (CDI) (for ages 7 to 17)
➤ Beck Depression Inventory (BDI) (for older teens)
➤ Center for Epidemiologic Studies Depression (CES-D) Scale

Subsequent Visits

At future visits, your parents will probably alternate between waiting for you outside and joining in the session as you and the therapist work on solving your problems and treating your depression. As you start work with your therapist, you may be surprised to find that it's not easy opening up and talking about uncomfortable feelings—especially with someone who's practically a stranger.

You also may be surprised to find out that sharing feelings isn't easy because many people don't spend much time thinking about exactly how they do feel. It can be hard to share your feelings if you aren't even sure what they are or why you're feeling sad or depressed.

That's why making a list of your feelings in between doctor visits can help. Don't just note the individual emotion ("angry" or "sad") but write down the situation in which you had the feelings: "Angry when Jed ignored me in school" or "Sad when I got up this morning. Have no idea why."

Once you've made your list, you can bring it along to your next appointment, and it may make things a bit easier. Sometimes kids have trouble putting their feelings into words. Here are some basic questions to get you started thinking about your sad feelings:

> ▸ Think back to a certain situation (your first date, your last birthday party, a family vacation, last night at the dinner table) and then think about how you were feeling.
> ▸ What is the first thought that came into your mind in that situation?
> ▸ What did you do when this situation occurred?
> ▸ How often do you feel this way?

You may have regular appointments once a week, a few times a week, or just once a month. No matter how often you meet, you should always feel comfortable when you meet with your therapist, who won't make you do anything you don't want to do or talk about anything you don't want to talk about.

Depending on the type of therapy you have, your therapist might ask you to set some goals, do "homework" outside the office, or keep a notebook describing your thoughts, actions, and feelings between visits. Bringing this notebook to your appointments can help you see whether you're starting to feel better.

SHOULD YOU TELL YOUR FRIENDS?

Whether you share with your friends that you're seeing a therapist is completely up to you. If you feel comfortable talking about it, then it's fine to let your friends know—after all, it's a big part of your life right now. If you'd rather keep that part of your life private, that's fine, too—as long as you realize there's nothing wrong with going to counseling. Some kids feel that getting this kind of help means they're crazy or too weak to figure out their own problems, but that's not true. Whether you have a physical illness like diabetes or the flu or an emotional problem like depression, it's smart to take charge and get help, and it's brave of you to admit you need help. There are lots of adults who aren't able to do that.

Remember, everybody has some kind of problem, and getting help for your depression will just make you get better that much faster.

IF YOU DON'T LIKE YOUR THERAPIST . . .

Therapists who choose a career of helping people are usually caring, sensitive individuals, but sometimes a therapist and a client just don't connect. You may have thought your therapist was terrific at first, but maybe your time together isn't progressing very well, and you may decide that you and your therapist just don't seem to be a good fit. After all, not everyone automatically gets along in any social relationship.

Your therapist understands this and won't take it personally. He or she also understands how important a good fit can be and may even suggest another therapist you might like better.

In any case, if you just don't feel comfortable with your current therapist, you are certainly within your rights to seek help elsewhere. Sometimes a person might need to visit several therapists before finding someone compatible—and that's perfectly okay.

If You're Thinking Of Harming Yourself...

Tell someone who can help right away or

- ▶ Call your doctor's office.
- ▶ Call 911 for emergency services.
- ▶ Go to the nearest hospital emergency room.

Call the toll-free, 24-hour hotline of the National Suicide Prevention Lifeline at **1-800-273-TALK (1-800-273-8255)** to be connected to a trained counselor at a suicide crisis center nearest you.

WHAT YOU NEED TO KNOW

- If you're feeling depressed, it's important to talk to someone you trust about your feelings.
- The government offers a state-by-state Mental Health Services Locator at http://www.mentalhealth.samhsa.gov/databases that provides information about mental health services and resources in each state.
- If you've been feeling depressed, check with a doctor first to make sure you don't have a physical illness that might be causing the symptoms.
- If you're in crisis, the local emergency room doctor can offer temporary help and can refer you to a mental health expert for further treatment.
- Psychologists, social workers, pastoral counselors, and psychiatrists all diagnose and treat mental health disorders.
- If you just don't feel comfortable with your current therapist, you can seek help elsewhere.

5

Treatment: Psychotherapy

"Snap out of it!"

"Quit moping around!"

"Just get up and start doing things and you'll feel better!"

Have you heard any of those comments before? If you're clinically depressed, chances are somebody's said something like this to you. But of course, people who are seriously depressed can't just "snap out of it" on their own. Nobody wants to be depressed. Depression isn't a moral failing or a personal weakness, either. It's an illness—a chemical imbalance in the brain—and almost everybody responds to treatment.

The good news is that you're not doomed to living with constant sadness, muffled in a gray fog. Your sad mood can be treated so that you can have a healthy, happy, and full life. Try not to be discouraged if some of your friends (or even family members) misunderstand your problem. People who don't understand depression may think you should be able to overcome your symptoms by sheer willpower. But as you know, these symptoms can't be wished away. (If it were that easy, you'd have wished them away a long time ago.) You can't just "snap out of it" just by wanting to feel better.

Of course, just because it's possible to treat depression doesn't mean it's easy. It can be a challenge to find the right treatment, and you'll have to be patient as your health care providers try to find just the right combination of psychotherapy and medication. But eventually, depression almost always responds well to a combination of therapy and medication.

Once your doctor has conducted a careful diagnostic exam to figure out exactly what your symptoms are and whether you have a mild or severe case of depression—or other conditions at the same time—it's time to start treatment. Remember that you and your therapist are a team, working together on your problems.

TYPES OF PSYCHOTHERAPY

If you've been diagnosed with depression, your health care provider has probably discussed treatment options, which ideally includes some kind of psychotherapy. Research has shown that short-term counseling along with medication is the very best kind of treatment for depression. But "talk therapy" doesn't mean you'll be lying on a couch analyzing your childhood for hours on end. There are different types of psychotherapy, but modern methods of treating depression are usually aimed at either changing your behavior (behavioral therapy) or changing your thoughts and your behavior (cognitive-behavioral therapy, or CBT).

In general, it's possible to say that during therapy, you'll explore events, beliefs, and feelings that you may find painful, and you'll learn how to develop new coping skills. Psychotherapy can help you identify the things that contribute to your depression and how to deal effectively with these psychological or behavioral problems and with

Substance Abuse: Do You Have a Problem?

Experts agree that if you are using alcohol or drugs, their use can interfere with treatment for your depression. If you can just stop, you should. If you cannot stop, you should tell your therapist and include this problem in your treatment. You might also consider participating in a self-help recovery program such as Alcoholics Anonymous (AA) or Narcotics Anonymous (NA). Once you conquer your drug or alcohol dependency, you'll have a much better chance of recovering from depression.

interpersonal relationships. You'll probably meet each week for about three months with a trained mental health professional (a psychiatrist, psychologist, social worker, or counselor) to learn how to deal with your depressive symptoms.

The aim of both CBT and behavioral therapy is for you to ease your depression by evaluating your beliefs and getting rid of behaviors that reinforce those feelings. Your therapist will work with you to pinpoint any problems that may have contributed to your depression and help you understand how you may be able to solve them. Your therapist can help you identify options and set realistic goals.

Your therapist also can help you identify distorted thinking patterns that contribute to feelings of hopelessness and helplessness that accompany depression, and he or she can help you nurture a more objective outlook on life. Common beliefs that cause problems are referred to as cognitive distortions. This might include "all-or nothing" thinking ("Not getting an 'A' it is the same as getting an 'F'!"), catastrophizing ("It's the worst thing that could ever happen!"), overgeneralization ("I'm the ugliest kid in my class"), and "should" or "must" statements ("I must get an A on my calculus quiz!"). Your therapist also will help you explore other learned thoughts and behaviors that create problems and contribute to depression and will help you improve the way you interact with other people. Sometimes, this type of therapy is conducted in a group setting of teens with similar problems. Eventually, your therapist can help you regain a sense of control and pleasure in life and help you slowly begin to enjoy activities again.

So how does it work? When you learn something new, the nerve cells in your brain form new connections. In much the same way, psychotherapy is effective in easing depression by actually changing the way the brain physically functions.

BEHAVIORAL THERAPY

Treating the behavior of a person who is depressed has been a popular method for many years. The basic idea behind behavioral theory is that what really counts is how you act. What's going on inside your head—your thoughts and beliefs—doesn't matter as much. If you feel miserable, this theory says, it's because of your behavior. That's why traditional behavioral therapists don't worry so much what you're thinking and instead focus on your behavior. A behavior therapist may teach you how to handle rejection or loss or how to behave to get along better with friends and family using social skills training or assertiveness training. The therapist may have you practice ways to respond to criticism as a way of desensitizing the effects of that criticism.

Changing your behavior can have dramatic results, but many modern experts believe that overcoming depression also requires some attention to your beliefs and thought processes. That's why cognitive ("thinking") therapy has become an added integral part of treatment for depression.

COGNITIVE-BEHAVIORAL THERAPY (CBT)

A cognitive therapist believes that your emotions are related to your thoughts and beliefs about yourself, other people, and the world and that you can be taught to recognize and react to stress and uncomfortable feelings in a healthy way.

If you take five minutes and monitor the thoughts that cross your mind, you'll be surprised at the constant flow of "chatter" that goes on. Some of these negative thoughts—called cognitive distortions—can disrupt your life and very subtly influence your outlook. It's the answer to that classic question: Is a glass of water half empty or half full? If you said "half empty," you see the glass as being incomplete and therefore not the perfect glass of water you require. Cognitive-behavioral therapy would work well for you if you think and behave in ways that trigger and perpetuate depression and if you have depression that significantly interferes with your life and causes suffering or interpersonal problems.

During a brief course of weekly discussions, the CB therapist would try to teach you how to evaluate your beliefs and develop alternative beliefs that lead to more positive life experiences. For example, if you think about something scary, you'll feel afraid. If you tend to think you're helpless to do anything about a situation, you're much more likely to be depressed. Cognitive-behavioral therapy trains you to identify those thought distortions that occur automatically, and challenge their validity.

For example, Sasha didn't want to go to her middle school dance. "Dances are stupid!" she says. "I don't like any of the boys who'll be there, and nobody will ask me to dance anyway. I feel like a dork!" Many vulnerable kids seem to develop a habit of viewing life this way from a kind of "depressed" filter. These kids enter adolescence convinced that they're not as good as others and there's nothing they can do about it. They tend to see the world in black-and-white terms, as an unfriendly place, and they tend to see their future as bleak.

In CBT, a major part of eliminating damaging automatic thoughts is to identify automatic, core beliefs and assumptions, and then develop alternative beliefs. This is a challenging task, because changing the way you think can mean undoing years of negative automatic thought patterns. A cognitive behavioral therapist wouldn't worry so much about why Sasha thinks she's a dork; he or she would just be interested in helping Sasha see herself more objectively and understand that she can control her situation.

This form of therapy focuses on healing unhelpful thought patterns—but it's much more than just positive thinking. A cognitive therapist might sit down with Sasha and try to help her understand how her fears may create the very reality she's worried about. The therapist then might help her learn new ways to think about herself and those boys she dismisses so easily. Their work together might include encouragement to take dance lessons, role playing, or repeating affirmations such as "I am confident and friendly" several times a day in front of a mirror. Research on children and adolescents with depression supports the idea that cognitive-behavioral therapy works well, although teens with severe or recurrent depression often need antidepressants.

Cognition The "cognitive" part of this treatment emphasizes identifying and then changing the problem thinking patterns that have kept you from overcoming your depression. The first step to addressing depression is to become aware of the thoughts and feelings that drive it. You'll be asked to monitor your mood changes each day so you can identify the first signs of discomfort. This will help you and the therapist figure out what specific situations at home or with friends are triggering these uncomfortable feelings. Actively investigating the thought processes from a cognitive point of view can dramatically affect your emotions and behavior.

Behavior The behavioral part of CBT focuses on changing your reactions to situations that might involve poor grades, poor performance, or having high standards and handling the stress that you may be feeling. Once you've monitored your mood changes and identified your triggers, you and the therapist can come up with different ideas for solving the problems. For example, if you feel sad because you don't have any friends, in behavior therapy you will learn the skills you need to get friends, such as how to have conversations, how to give and receive compliments and criticism, how to increase intimacy, and how to tolerate the discomfort caused by increased intimacy. If your grades are poor, in behavior therapy you can learn to develop better study habits, stay focused, and set priorities to help you achieve your goal of having better grades. One approach might involve helping you understand the worst thing that could happen if you don't do well. Having a client consider the worst that could happen helps clarify the truth of a situation. You might be asked to test new ways of thinking or acting about the things that generate depression. Or you might learn to tolerate situations that have caused discomfort in the past. During your treatment, your therapist will probably assign homework—specific problems that you'll need to work on between sessions.

INTERPERSONAL THERAPY

This is a type of short-term therapy that focuses exclusively on social relationships with others. Are you timid or assertive, shy or aggressive? Do you have good social skills? Are you the life of the party, or do you sit in the back row along the wall, hoping no one will notice you? No matter what, many depressed kids and teens aren't happy with their relationships—their friends, their families, or their teachers. One of the biggest problems that these depressed kids experience is a problem with social skills. Maybe you don't know what to say, so you hang back and don't say anything. Do you look at the floor when someone talks to you? Do you keep your mouth shut when everyone else in the group is laughing and chatting? Do you ask too many questions, or get loud and silly when that cute boy walks by? Do you talk about yourself too much—or not at all? Have you never learned the give-and-take of small talk? Interpersonal therapy (IPT) can help you with all of these skills, giving you a practical, sensible guideline to learn better social and communication skills.

Many teens develop depression during a time when they need to be making major life choices relating to education, friends, values, and family relationships. Interpersonal therapy can help you develop better ways to deal with these issues, which may have been linked to the onset of your depression. This can help prevent recurrent episodes of depression in the future. Interpersonal therapy works well in treating depression, and for teenagers it typically lasts for up to 12 sessions (usually once a week for an hour per session). During a session, your therapist will typically focus on one or two key issues that seem to be most closely related to your depression. Normally, your parents will be asked to participate in the initial and final phases of treatment. During the first sessions, your therapist will teach your parents about depression and about treatment procedures, emphasizing the need for family support. Your parents may be asked to participate in the middle sessions if there are any communication problems between you and your family. Your parents will then be invited to participate in the final sessions to discuss your progress, changes in the family as a result of treatment, and the need for further or future treatment.

Although depression may not be caused specifically by the way you relate to your parents, depression usually does affect relationships with other people and the roles you play in those relationships. That's why a combination of therapy and medication works so well for depression—the medication can treat the physical side of the depression, but the therapy helps with all of the interpersonal issues that have been created because you are depressed.

During treatment, your therapist will focus on interpersonal events that seem to have been responsible either for triggering or maintaining your depression, such as personal conflicts, your role in your family or with your friends, complicated grief, and so on. For the first couple of sessions, your therapist will try to identify your specific interpersonal issues, which the two of you will focus on for the rest of therapy.

Although IPT isn't always effective, research has shown that it's just as effective in the short-term treatment of depression as antidepressants are. Since people who have been depressed are at risk for having new bouts of depression in the future, successful short-term treatment may be combined with ongoing therapy. In one recent study, people with recurrent major depression who received interpersonal therapy and antidepressants for three years were much less likely to have a recurrence than those who received only medication or only counseling. This is called maintenance IPT, and your therapist may suggest that you meet once a month after you've ended your initial therapy sessions. Research suggests that by doing this, you may be able to postpone the recurrence of depression.

GROUP THERAPY

Group psychotherapy is a special form of therapy in which a small number of people meet with a professionally trained therapist. This type of therapy has been a standard treatment option for more than 50 years. Many people do very well in group psychotherapy because it allows them to share with others who have similar problems or concerns. This can help you better understand your own situation as you learn from and with one another.

If you're depressed, group therapy can help you learn about yourself and improve relationships with other people as you work on your feelings of anxiety, isolation, and depression. Working in a group can help you make changes in your life that will make you feel better about yourself, too.

Scientists who have studied group therapy have discovered that this method is just as effective as traditional psychotherapy—and sometimes may even be more effective. Many experts believe that the best way to deal with depression is to combine medication, individual psychotherapy, and group therapy. Your therapist can talk with you so that you understand the benefits of each of these treatments and help you determine what will work best for you.

Group psychotherapists can be psychiatrists, psychologists, social workers, psychiatric nurses, pastoral counselors, marriage and family therapists, or substance abuse counselors. If you're thinking about joining a group, you or your parents should make sure the person is qualified. Look for the "CGP" designation after the therapist's name—that's the signal that the person has received special training in group therapy and been certified by the National Registry of Certified Group Psychotherapists. Clinical members of the American Group Psychotherapy Association (AGPA) also have received specialized training.

A typical group session lasts about 75 to 90 minutes. During the meeting, you'll work on expressing your own ideas, problems, and feelings as honestly as you can. The more honest you are, the better the group will be able to help. As each of the members talks about feelings and how he or she acts on those feelings, the group learns how to understand themselves and their own issues as well. In the process, they often learn how to help one another, too.

A therapist puts together a group of about five to 10 clients who he or she thinks might get something out of a group experience. Group members may not all have the exact same problem. While some members probably will be depressed, all the members may not feel this way. This can be a good thing, since people with different problems can bring a range of strengths and insights to the group.

Moreover, not all groups are alike. One group may focus on having members help one another; another group might spend most of its time helping members learn how to control thoughts (sort of like cognitive therapy) or how to handle situations that trigger depression. But whatever the group's focus, during the meeting you'll be encouraged to talk with one another openly and honestly. Your therapist will help examine all of the problems and feelings affecting the individuals and the group and will guide the discussions.

Your therapist may want to use group therapy as the only treatment for you, though most therapists like to combine group and individual therapy. Many teens discover that working in both group and individual therapy at the same time can help a lot. Your therapist may run your group, or he or she may refer you to a colleague's group. If that's your case, the two therapists will communicate with each other about your progress.

Group therapy is different from self-help or support groups. In group therapy, you'll learn how to cope with your problems but also how to change behavior and grow as an individual. *Support groups* are not necessarily led by professionals, but these groups usually focus on easing symptoms and helping people cope with difficult situations. *Self-help groups* usually focus on a particular symptom or situation shared by all the members of the group and usually aren't led by a trained therapist.

If your therapist has suggested that you join a group, you may have some worries or concerns. After all, it's one thing to talk about your problems to your therapist, but teens can sometimes feel uncomfortable about sharing their personal thoughts in a room full of strangers. You may worry: *What if I don't like the people in my group?* Of course, it's perfectly natural to feel a bit anxious when you first join, but most teens soon begin to thaw out and start to trust their fellow group members. In fact, you'll probably feel at ease and relieved when you realize you'll have the chance to talk with other kids with the same problems.

In joining a group, you'll have the opportunity to learn from other people. If you've ever gotten together casually with a bunch of close friends and ended up talking about a problem you have—only to find out many of your friends have the same problem—you know how supportive it can be to share this experience. That's what group therapy is like, too—with the added benefit of a trained leader guiding the conversation.

In group therapy, you'll learn that you may not be as different (or as hopeless) as you think you are. You'll discover that you're not alone and that you're not the only person who feels the way you do. And remember, the more involved you are with the group, the more you'll get out of it.

How long a group lasts depends on the type of group and the extent of your problems. Short-term groups devoted to specific issues may last from six to 20 weeks, but in an open-ended group, you can leave whenever you've reached your goals. You should talk to your therapist to determine the length of time that's right for you.

Typically, group therapy costs about half as much as individual therapy, although this can vary depending on where you live and the type of therapist you have. Most managed care insurance companies cover group therapy the same as individual therapy.

OUTLOOK

All psychotherapy treatments for depression—whether CBT, interpersonal therapy, group therapy, or behavioral techniques—try to help you see that you can control your mind, your body, and your life. Treatments are highly effective and greatly improve the quality of your life. But this kind of treatment will work best if you attend all of your scheduled appointments. How effective it is will depend on how actively you participate and whether you're willing to work with your therapist to deal with your depression. People who actively participate in therapy recover faster than those who aren't motivated. They also have fewer relapses. Of course, you'll need to spend time evaluating your thoughts and behavior, and you'll have to think carefully to identify stresses that contribute to your depression. Then you'll need to work on improving these areas. All of this takes time; therapy isn't a quick fix.

When you first start therapy, you and your therapist will probably establish some goals. As you work together, you should periodically review your progress. If you don't like your therapist's approach or if you don't think he or she is helping, you should talk this out. You can always ask your parents to let you seek a second opinion, but you shouldn't just quit therapy abruptly without talking about the problems you're having.

WHAT YOU NEED TO KNOW

- ▸ You can't just "snap out of" depression by wanting to feel better.
- ▸ Depression almost always responds well to a combination of therapy and medication.
- ▸ Depression is treated either by changing behavior (behavioral therapy) or changing thoughts and behavior (cognitive-behavioral therapy, or CBT).
- ▸ Psychotherapy can help you identify what contributes to your depression and how to deal effectively with these psychological or behavioral problems and with interpersonal relationships
- ▸ Interpersonal therapy is a type of short-term therapy that focuses on how you communicate with and relate to others.
- ▸ Group psychotherapy is a special form of therapy in which a small number of people meet with a professionally trained therapist.

6

Treatment: Antidepressants

Sandy didn't remember exactly when she started to feel depressed—it all happened so gradually. Mostly, she felt numb and increasingly distant from everyone and everything around her. Her parents divorced when she was just three, and she'd been living with her father ever since. Her father had hoped that she would "snap out of it," but as weeks and months dragged on, he became more and more concerned. "Maybe she's just moody," he told himself. "After all, she's a teenager. Isn't that how teenagers act?"

Finally, Sandy's counselor at school suggested to her father that Sandy's problems were not just normal teenage moodiness. The counselor thought Sandy might be depressed and recommended that she see a therapist. The therapist agreed that Sandy was depressed and recommended a combination of psychotherapy and a course of antidepressants.

Sandy's father was unhappy about the idea of medication at first, but the therapist convinced him Sandy wasn't lazy or willful. She really had a medical problem that required medication as a helpful short-term boost while she worked on getting better.

HOW ANTIDEPRESSANTS WORK

Although there have been many theories about the cause of depression over the years, most experts today place the origin of the problem in the brain. Neurons use chemical messengers called neurotransmitters to communicate with one another. The chemicals

51

are released at the end of one nerve cell, carrying a message as they move across the gap between that nerve cell and the next and changing the membrane of the second nerve cell so that it fires, sending the message on its way. Most experts believe that people become depressed when the levels of certain chemicals drop too low, so that messages can't cross the gaps between brain cells (neurons) and communication in the brain slows down. There are at least 100 types of neurotransmitters in the brain, but those that seem to be most related to depression are serotonin, norepinephrine, and dopamine. Antidepressant drugs boost the levels of these chemicals, thereby easing depression.

One class of drugs, selective serotonin reuptake inhibitors (SSRIs), focus on just one neurotransmitter: serotonin. In the past decade, research studies of serotonin have found that it plays an essential role in the regulation of emotion, sleep, appetite, temperature, blood vessel tone, secretion of certain hormones, and the perception of pain. It appears to play a particularly strong role in the development of depression.

After serotonin is released in the brain, it is reabsorbed by the brain cells so that it can be used again later. This reabsorbing is called reuptake. If you're feeling depressed, you may not have enough serotonin; if the serotonin that you have is prevented from being reabsorbed, more remains available in your brain to send messages. A drug that only affects the reuptake of serotonin is selective—and that's where the name SSRI comes from.

The SSRIs are popular because they only affect serotonin. Older antidepressants affected many different neurotransmitters, and the more chemicals and systems that are affected in the brain, the more side effects you tend to have. SSRIs are so selective that they leave most of the brain's chemicals and processes alone. If a light switch in your house stopped working, you wouldn't ask your electrician to rip out all of the electrical wiring in the entire house—you'd just replace the one switch. Treating depression is much the same thing. There's no need to disrupt neurotransmitters firing all over the brain if the problem is only with serotonin—but for many years, the older antidepressants did just that. That's because scientists didn't know how to design an antidepressant that would focus on just the light switch and leave all the other electrical wiring alone. Yet some people do seem to become depressed just from the neurological equivalent of one light switch—just low levels of one neurotransmitter. For years, scientists searched for this one-chemical antidepressant, and they finally found it when they discovered Prozac.

That doesn't mean that the serotonin system is simple—in fact, it is an extremely complex system of interwoven connections that produce the chemical all over the brain. Serotonin receptors tend to cluster in parts of the brain having to do with emotion, and there are at least six receptor types in the serotonin system, each sending different signals to different parts of the brain. Although scientists have figured out that serotonin is linked to emotion and depression, it may be far from a straightforward relationship. It may be that boosting serotonin levels simply improves depression, but it could also be that affecting the levels of serotonin causes mild effects in other neurotransmitter systems throughout the brain and that those changes influence emotion and depression.

After Prozac became available in 1988, more medications in the same SSRI group became available soon after: Paxil, Zoloft, and Luvox appeared in the mid-1990s, followed by Celexa in 1998. SSRIs aren't the only choice to treat depression, however. Between 20 and 40 percent of depressed people don't respond to these drugs. Many of these people instead find relief with some of the newer, structurally unrelated drugs such as Wellbutrin, Effexor, or Desyrel or the old standbys—the tricyclics or the monoamine oxidase inhibitors (MAOIs).

THE STIGMA OF MEDICATION

Pills may not cure the problem itself, any more than a Band-Aid heals a cut, but your body can heal itself, given the right support. Medications can keep your symptoms under control and help you lead a normal, fulfilling life while your body heals. It can be an important treatment for depression in adolescents, especially when combined with individual psychotherapy to boost the effectiveness of medication and to help lessen the risk of suicidal thoughts or behaviors.

Unfortunately, some people still think that taking medication means they're weak. Some kids say they don't want to be dependent on a pill. As a result, sometimes these people don't take their medications, even though antidepressants can play an important role in a self-help program. Or they take too little of the drug, mistakenly believing that less is better. Or they stop taking an effective medication too quickly, assuming that they are cured, or skip days and only take a pill when the depression seems especially bad. What they don't realize is that taking medication incorrectly is just as bad (and sometimes worse) than not taking anything at all. The only way that medication can really help is if you take it exactly as the doctor prescribes, every single day.

GETTING THE RIGHT DOSE

If your doctor prescribes an antidepressant, you'll probably start off with a low dose that will be gradually increased until you reach what's called the therapeutic level—the dose that best eases your symptoms. Don't expect a dramatic difference right away. Taking an antidepressant isn't like taking an aspirin for a headache—you can't expect your depressed mood to disappear instantly after the first dose. Most people take antidepressants for several weeks before they notice that they are starting to feel better. In the meantime, it's important not to get discouraged and stop taking your medicine before it has a chance to work.

Remember that there is one specific dose that will be best for you, and your physician will help identify what that amount may be. Psychiatrists or other physicians can prescribe medications for depression, and they often work closely with psychologists, social workers, or counselors who provide psychotherapy. (In New Mexico and Louisiana, specially trained psychologists can prescribe medication on their own.) Work with your doctor in the beginning of your treatment as he or she adjusts the dose gradually. Most physicians will begin a drug at a low dose and then increase it slowly according to your response. You must take a drug for several weeks at full dose to figure out whether it works or not.

Most antidepressants are not approved by the FDA for kids under age 18, but doctors routinely prescribe these medications to young patients. This practice, called off-label use, is common for many illnesses and perfectly legal.

Once your symptoms are under control, your doctor will probably suggest that you can begin to taper your medication—this will usually take up to 12 to 18 months, depending on your condition. As you gradually stop taking your medications, some of your symptoms may return. After about one month, your doctor probably will assess how well you're doing without medication. If it's not going well, you can always discuss taking the drug again—or trying a different one. Sometimes, a doctor may decide that long-term medication is the best treatment.

TYPES OF ANTIDEPRESSANTS

If you've been diagnosed with depression, odds are that your doctor will prescribe a combination of psychotherapy and an antidepressant

If You Run Out of Medication . . .

If you're taking a medication that could cause problems if you suddenly stop taking it and you run out of pills and can't get a refill, go to your local emergency room. Some medications can cause very difficult withdrawals.

medication, just like Sandy was given. There are several types of antidepressants:

> selective serotonin reuptake inhibitors (SSRIs)
> serotonin norepinephrine reuptake inhibitors (SNRIs)
> chemically unrelated miscellaneous antidepressants
> tricyclics
> monoamine oxidase inhibitors (MAOIs)

Because different antidepressants work better for some people than others, the first one you try may not be the best choice for you. In fact, between 30 and 40 percent of kids don't respond to the first medication, but they do improve on the next medication their doctor tries. Your doctor may need to switch prescriptions several times before finding the medication that most effectively eases your symptoms. The important thing is not to give up before finding just the right medication that can improve your symptoms.

*A **word about side effects.*** Each type of antidepressant has different side effects, but in general the newer SSRIs and SNRIs have fewer side effects and are less dangerous in overdose than the tricyclics and MAOIs more commonly used in the past. Usually these side effects are minor; they may be irritating, but they don't require medical attention. These side effects may also diminish or end in a few days or weeks as your body adjusts to the medication. Before using one of these medications, ask your doctor about possible side effects—what you can expect, what might get better as time passes, and which side effects you need to report immediately.

Some doctors don't like to discuss side effects, because it's hard to know which patients will experience them, and doctors worry that bringing up the subject may make you more inclined to experience them. On the other hand, if you don't know what to expect, any side effects can be scary. If you know what to expect, you can prepare yourself to deal with it. Often these minor problems improve over a few weeks as your body adjusts or if the dosage is lowered. In the meantime, you can handle these effects by sucking on a hard candy for dry mouth, getting a new glasses prescription for blurred vision, or eating more bran, fruits, and vegetables to combat constipation.

Suicide risk. You may have heard about recent concerns linking certain SSRIs with teenage suicide. First, remember that there is no evidence that antidepressants increase the risk of completed suicide, but there is plenty of evidence that untreated depression significantly increases an adolescent's risk for suicide. Not all suicidal kids are depressed, and very rarely does a depressed teen die as a result of a suicide attempt. Nonetheless, kids with a mood disorder such as

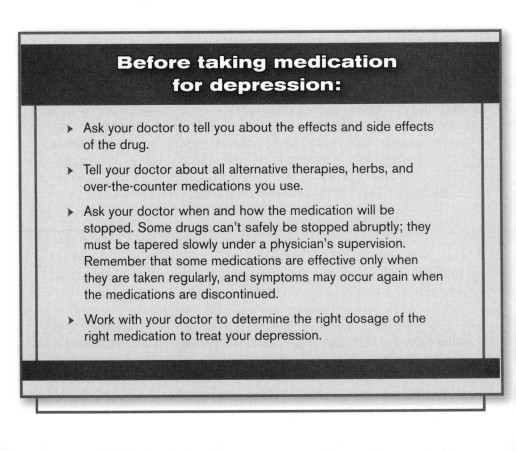

Before taking medication for depression:

▸ Ask your doctor to tell you about the effects and side effects of the drug.

▸ Tell your doctor about all alternative therapies, herbs, and over-the-counter medications you use.

▸ Ask your doctor when and how the medication will be stopped. Some drugs can't safely be stopped abruptly; they must be tapered slowly under a physician's supervision. Remember that some medications are effective only when they are taken regularly, and symptoms may occur again when the medications are discontinued.

▸ Work with your doctor to determine the right dosage of the right medication to treat your depression.

depression are five times more likely to attempt suicide than those who aren't depressed.

The U.S. Food and Drug Administration (FDA) issued a warning in October 2004 that antidepressant medications (including SSRIs) may increase suicidal thoughts and suicide attempts in a small number of children and adolescents, and it required antidepressant manufacturers to include labels with strong warnings on their products. The warning labels apply to all antidepressants, even though the FDA analysis only examined nine drugs.

The FDA report was based on a review of 24 brief studies of nine antidepressants involving more than 4,400 children and adolescents with major depressive disorder, obsessive-compulsive disorder, or other psychiatric disorders. The studies showed that the average risk of suicidal thoughts and attempts occurred in 4 percent of patients treated with an antidepressant, compared with 2 percent of patients treated with a sugar pill. No actual suicides occurred in any of the studies. There was some evidence that suicidal thoughts and behaviors occurred most often at the beginning of treatment or when the dosage was changed. However, this doesn't mean a problem couldn't appear later in treatment.

Doctors don't really know why this happened, but there are several possible reasons. First, some kids who are given antidepressants may have an undiagnosed bipolar disorder. Treating these kids with antidepressants could cause an episode of mania that leads to risky, impulsive behavior, including self-harm. (See Chapter 2.) In addition, some scientists suspect that a few kids may attempt suicide at the beginning of antidepressant treatment because the medication finally gives them the energy to act on deep-seated feelings of hopelessness, sadness, or worthlessness—before the antidepressants have had time to ease those feelings.

But research also shows that the treatment of depression with antidepressant medication is linked to an overall decrease in the risk of suicide. Data collected by the Centers for Disease Control and Prevention (CDC) show that between 1992 and 2001, the rate of suicide among American kids aged 10 to 19 dropped by more than 25 percent, while there was a significant increase in antidepressant prescriptions for this age group. In fact, the dramatic drop in youth suicide rates correlates with the increased rates of prescribing SSRIs.

Newer studies further refine this information. A 2006 study concludes that youths who use certain antidepressants—but not most SSRIs—are more likely to attempt suicide, according to the report in the August *Archives of General Psychiatry.* In that study, researchers found that those who had attempted suicide were 1.5 times more likely to have been taking an antidepressant and 15 times more likely to die in the attempt than those not treated with an antidepressant. In particular, kids who used antidepressants seemed to be at higher risk for suicide in the period after being hospitalized, especially if they were just starting to take antidepressants. However, not all types of antidepressants carried the same risk.

Venlafaxine (Effexor)—a serotonin-norepinephrine reuptake inhibitor (SNRI)—was associated with 2.3 times the risk of suicide attempts compared with no drug treatment at all. Tricyclic antidepressants were also significantly linked with suicide attempts. But with the exception of Zoloft, SSRIs weren't linked to suicide attempts, the study found.

Are you at risk? Some kids are at higher risk of suicide attempts whether they're taking antidepressants or not. You're at higher risk for suicide if you

- have depression, bipolar disorder, or anxiety
- have already attempted suicide
- abuse drugs or alcohol
- are related to someone who is depressed or has tried to commit suicide
- have had a history of sexual or physical abuse
- have been exposed to violence
- are under social stress and isolation
- have access to guns

Your doctor will assess your risks as part of the treatment evaluation. The FDA warning doesn't forbid you to use these medications. It's just a warning that while for most kids antidepressants lower the risk of suicide, for a very small number there is a slightly higher risk in the first few days of a new prescription. That's why you and your parents need to be aware of suicidal thoughts and behaviors when you first go on medication.

If your doctor prescribes an antidepressant for you, you should personally meet with the doctor at least once a week for the first four weeks of treatment. You can cut these in-person appointments to twice a month during the second month of treatment, and then monthly after that.

What to watch out for. Once you start taking an antidepressant, you and your family should be on the lookout for any changes in behavior. You should see a doctor right away if you or your family, friends, or teachers notice any of the following:

> suicidal thoughts
> suicide attempts
> worsening depression
> anxiety
> feelings of severe agitation or restlessness or panic attacks
> insomnia
> new or worsening irritability
> aggression, anger, or violence
> acting on dangerous impulses
> extreme hyperactivity (mania)
> other unusual changes in behavior

SELECTIVE SEROTONIN REUPTAKE INHIBITORS

If you're diagnosed with depression, your doctor is most likely to first prescribe one of the newest antidepressants with the big name: selective serotonin reuptake inhibitors (SSRIs). These include the following:

> Prozac, Prozac Weekly (fluoxetine)
> Celexa (citalopram)
> Zoloft (sertraline)
> Luvox (fluvoxamine)
> Paxil, Paxil CR (paroxetine)
> Lexapro (escitalopram oxalate)

You probably know these drugs by one of the brand names—Prozac. More than 10 million people have taken Prozac alone for depression, and more than 70 percent of them have gotten better. The SSRIs boost

If You're Thinking about Suicide . . .

If you're taking an antidepressant and you start thinking about suicide or you suddenly feel agitated, restless, and irritable, you should tell your parents and contact your doctor immediately. The medication dose may need to be changed. But remember, you shouldn't stop taking your medication without a doctor's supervision since this may worsen symptoms.

levels of the brain chemical messenger serotonin, which helps control mood and emotions.

Prozac is the one SSRI that has been officially approved to be given to kids for their depression, but many doctors may start with one of the other SSRIs instead, depending on symptoms. For example, some kids sleep all the time when they are depressed, so an SSRI like Prozac, which can sometimes give you more energy, is a good idea. Other kids can't sleep at all when they're depressed, so a better choice for this group would be a more sedating SSRI. Your doctor will take into account exactly how you're feeling when choosing which medication to try.

These drugs are so popular because they work as well as any of the older antidepressants, but without all the side effects. Many SSRIs also are used to treat other kinds of problems, including obsessive-compulsive disorder, social phobia, anxiety or panic disorders, post-traumatic stress disorder, eating disorders, and PMS.

Although all SSRIs are equally effective, your unique chemical makeup and how depressed you are can affect how the drug works. In addition, some drugs stay in your body longer than others. Some SSRIs are available in extended-release forms or controlled-release forms, often designated with the letters XR or CR. These forms, which aren't suitable for everyone, are intended to provide controlled release of the medication throughout the day or for a week at a time with a single dose. The problem with extended relief drugs is that if you have a problem with side effects, it will take longer for the drug to leave your system.

General side effects. SSRIs have fewer side effects than older antidepressants, but that doesn't mean they don't have any side effects at all. Before you start taking one of these medications, be sure to ask your doctor what kinds of side effects to expect. That way, you won't be scared if you suddenly start feeling nervous, jumpy, tired, or nauseated. Luckily, those symptoms usually disappear with time; extended relief medications can help with nausea. Other symptoms might include sexual problems, including reduced desire or orgasm difficulties; headache; diarrhea; rash; increased sweating; weight gain; drowsiness; or insomnia.

The primary difference among the SSRIs is the side effects they produce. Paxil produces the most drowsiness, so if you have insomnia this could be the best choice for you. Zoloft and Luvox seem to cause more stomach upsets such as nausea or diarrhea. Paxil, Prozac, and Zoloft seem to make people less interested in eating, but Luvox doesn't affect appetite. Paxil has been linked to more complaints with dry mouth and constipation and seems to trigger more pronounced withdrawal symptoms. All the SSRIs appear to cause at least some problems with sexual interest or performance.

If the side effects really bother you, your doctor may be able to adjust the dose or switch to another SSRI to correct the problem. It's important to discuss side effects with your doctor so that he or she will know when a change in medication is needed.

Luckily, these drugs—unlike lithium or older antidepressants—do not seem to be very dangerous, even in high doses. (One patient who took more than 3,000 mg of Prozac survived without lasting damage.)

Serotonin syndrome. A rare but potentially life-threatening side effect of SSRIs is called serotonin syndrome, indicating that there is a dangerously high level of serotonin in the brain. This can happen if you take an SSRI and another type of antidepressant called a monoamine oxidase inhibitor (MAOI) at the same time. It also can happen if you take an SSRI with other medications or supplements that affect serotonin levels, such as the antidepression herb St. John's wort, or an antismoking patch (bupropion). Symptoms of serotonin syndrome include confusion, hallucinations, extreme agitation, fluctuations in blood pressure and heart rhythm, fever, seizures, and coma. Serotonin syndrome is a medical emergency that requires immediate medical treatment.

Interactions. All SSRIs interact in much the same way with other drugs. The most serious is a possible interaction with the antidepressant class of MAOIs. For this reason, you must allow at least two weeks between stopping a drug from one class before starting a drug from the other. If you've been taking Prozac, you should wait at least five weeks after stopping Prozac before taking an MAOI.

Drug combinations. Sometimes your doctor may want to combine two types of antidepressants to better help you cope with symptoms. For example, Desyrel may be added to Prozac if you're having trouble sleeping while taking Prozac.

Withdrawal. Although SSRIs aren't addictive, if you quit taking them suddenly after being on the medication for at least six weeks, you can experience withdrawal-like symptoms (a condition called antidepressant discontinuation syndrome), which include flulike symptoms, sensory disturbances, headache, dizziness, and lethargy.

You should never abruptly stop taking antidepressant medications because of the possibility of withdrawal effects such as agitation or increased depression. You should always talk to your doctor before changing or stopping your medication.

This syndrome occurs in about 20 percent of patients who suddenly stop their SSRI medication, so talk to your doctor before you do so.

Prozac

Studies suggest that younger kids respond to very small doses, as little as 5 to 10 mg, to begin. In fact, many kids who don't respond to other antidepressants do respond to Prozac. Prozac doesn't seem to cause the heart problems in kids that may occur with some antidepressants. Prozac Weekly is available as a once-a-week drug for patients who have been successfully taking the daily medication. Available as a 90-mg extended release pill, it's cheaper and easier to take.

Whatever version you take, you should expect results within two to three weeks, although a few people insist they begin to notice improvement within one week. You should take Prozac for at least six months before assuming it won't work. If you do start to feel better when taking this medication, most experts believe you should continue taking it for six to eight months before stopping. When you and your doctor decide it's time to stop, your doctor will explain to you how you can tell if your depression is returning.

Prozac does not usually cause problems when you stop taking it, even if you abruptly stop. Nevertheless, some doctors prefer that you slowly taper off the drug and watch for any indication that your depression is coming back. Your depression could be returning if you start to feel lethargic or you start to have some low moods. If you and your doctor decide your depression is returning, you can just start taking your Prozac again, and it should work as well as it did before.

You need to be prepared for the fact that if you do improve and go off Prozac, there's a 50 percent chance that your depression will return someday. If you've already had two episodes of depression, the chance of a third episode rises to 90 percent. That's why some experts recommend that people with recurrent depression take Prozac indefinitely.

Side effects. The problem most kids notice when they take Prozac is restlessness and sweating. Older people notice nausea with this medication, but younger kids don't seem to have such a problem with this. If you do feel sick to your stomach when you take this drug, the nausea should stop within about two weeks. It can help to take your medication with food or (if your doctor approves) to divide the dose in half for a while. If your nausea doesn't improve or go away after a week or two, your doctor may want to switch you to another antidepressant.

Prozac also often causes people to feel nervous or jumpy—almost as if you've drunk too many cups of coffee. The stimulatory effects of Prozac can make it hard for some people to sleep, but only a small percentage of people find it so difficult that they have to stop taking the drug. It may help to take Prozac earlier in the day, or ask your doctor about combining it with Desyrel, which has a more sedating effect. Oddly enough, another small group of people get very sleepy when taking Prozac.

A few individuals also notice dry mouth, sweating, tremors, or rash when taking Prozac. Up to 70 percent of people notice sexual problems, including delayed ejaculation, impotence, decreased interest, or problems reaching orgasm.

The one difference between Prozac and other SSRIs is that Prozac stays in your body much longer—up to six weeks after you stop taking it. This means that if you have an unpleasant reaction to this drug, the symptoms may linger long after you've stopped taking it. On the positive side, this means that if you forget a dose, you'll be less likely to have withdrawal symptoms.

Food and drug interactions. Prozac does not interact with any foods or beverages; taking it with food or milk can help ease the nausea this drug may cause. You can take Prozac with nonprescription medications such as Advil or Tylenol, and you also can combine (with your doctor's okay) Prozac and Valium. Prozac mixed with tricyclics also isn't dangerous, although side effects may be enhanced. But as described above, you should never mix Prozac with an MAOI antidepressant such as Nardil or Parnate. This can cause a fatal reaction involving high blood pressure and shock.

Special concerns. Be sure to tell your doctor if you have problems with your liver or kidneys, because with these problems, Prozac could build up in your blood. You also should be cautious about taking Prozac if you have a history of epilepsy or if you're taking antiseizure medication. If you have this sort of history, your doctor will give you lots of neurological tests and an EEG before prescribing. You'll also probably need to take smaller-than-average doses to begin and have blood tests during treatment.

Celexa

Celexa was approved in 1998 as a treatment for depression, and has been well tolerated among the more than 8 million people who have taken it around the world. In addition, it is less expensive than some other SSRIs. Celexa is taken once a day in the morning or evening, with or without food, typically beginning with a 20-mg dose. This can be increased to 40 mg if needed.

Side effects. Side effects with this medication typically are mild and don't last very long. You may notice dry mouth, diarrhea, tremor, insomnia, or sleepiness. A few people notice low blood pressure, dizziness when standing up, rapid heartbeat, headache, weight loss or gain, confusion, coughing, rash, itching, or taste problems. Celexa also interferes with many aspects of sexual function and interest.

Food and drug interactions. You should not drink and take Celexa, and you should discuss with your doctor any nonprescription medicines you take. Some drugs affect the way Celexa works in the body, including cimetidine (which raises the blood level of Celexa); antifungal drugs and the antibiotic erythromycin may slow down Celexa's clearance from the body. Celexa doubles the concentration of a metabolite of the tricyclic antidepressant imipramine, and you should never combine Celexa with any MAOI.

Special concerns. You should tell your doctor if you have mania, seizures, or liver or kidney disease. Celexa stays in the body twice as long in patients with liver problems, so lower doses will probably be recommended if you have this problem.

Zoloft

This drug has been approved for the treatment of major depression as well as panic disorder, post-traumatic stress disorder, and obsessive-compulsive disorder. Most people with depression are started at a dose of 50 mg; if you don't feel any better after a few weeks, the doctor may boost the dose and reassess your condition. Severely depressed individuals may need up to 200 mg a day to feel better. The drug may take up to two days to leave the body.

Side effects. One of the first side effects that people notice with this drug may be fatigue; other side effects may include insomnia, diarrhea, tremor, and dizziness. Nausea and irritated stomach may occur but can be avoided if you take the drug with food or beverages. Severe nausea should be discussed with your doctor. The risk of death from overdose is very low. Zoloft also may cause problems with sexual function.

Zoloft may trigger a very mild mania in people who already have that tendency. Others notice a small loss of appetite and subsequent weight loss with this medication. Very rarely, there have been reports of abnormal bleeding and purple skin spots or very low sodium levels (a condition called hyponatremia).

Food and drug interactions. Although Zoloft's manufacturers don't recommend mixing this medication with alcohol, it does not appear to cause a problem when the two are used together. There are no known dangerous reactions between nonprescription drugs and Zoloft, but you should be sure to talk to your doctor about any other medications you take. Combining Zoloft with either digitoxin or warfarin (Coumadin) may cause side effects. And as with all SSRIs, you should never combine Zoloft with any MAOI. If you've been using Zoloft for more than three months, you should not take an MAOI until at least three weeks have passed after your last Zoloft dose.

You can take Zoloft with food or beverages, although eating or drinking anything may harmlessly increase the blood level of Zoloft.

Special concerns. If you have liver disease, you should not take Zoloft, and anyone with a history of seizures should use this drug carefully.

Luvox
Luvox was approved in 1994 as a treatment for obsessive-compulsive disorder for adults; it was approved specifically to treat obsessive-compulsive disorder in children and teens in 1997. Although not specifically approved to treat depression, it's widely used for that condition.

Most doctors begin with 25 mg for kids aged 8 to 17, gradually increasing by 25 mg every four to seven days. A typical dose is between 50 and 200 mg daily; daily doses above 50 mg should be divided into two doses (morning and evening). You should expect to wait from two to four weeks before noticing improvement, although it may take as long as two months before you really respond to this drug. The drug is not approved for kids under age 8.

Side effects. Nausea and stomach upset are common, so you should take this drug with food or beverages. The risk of death with this drug when taken in overdose is extremely low. Luvox can trigger a mild mania in some people who already have such a tendency. Other common side effects include drowsiness or insomnia, headache, weakness, dry mouth, dizziness or nervousness, constipation, appetite loss, and weight loss. Luvox also may affect sexual interest and function. Very rarely, Luvox has been linked to seizures in people with a history of seizures.

Food and drug interactions. Celexa with warfarin (Coumadin) boosts the blood levels of warfarin; combining Celexa with tryptophan may lead to restlessness, insomnia, anxiety, and stomach problems. Luvox also may boost the blood levels of a variety of other drugs, including Tegretol, lithium, tricyclics, Inderal, Lopressor, methadone, and caffeine. Of course, you should never combine Luvox and MAOIs; if you've used Luvox for more than three months, you should not start an MAOI until three weeks after your last Luvox dose.

Special concerns. Anyone with severe kidney or liver disease should discuss this with a doctor before taking Luvox, since these conditions can keep Luvox in the body for up to 30 percent longer.

Paxil

Paxil was approved to treat depression and a variety of other mental conditions, including social anxiety and generalized anxiety disorder. Patients with depression usually begin with 20 mg a day, which may be increased to 50 mg daily if there is no improvement. The risk of overdose with this medication is very low.

Side effects. Most side effects are mild and include fatigue or insomnia, nausea, headache, dizziness or lightheadedness, and dry mouth. Paxil also can trigger mild mania in some people who have that tendency. Some people may notice a loss of appetite and corresponding mild weight loss; others eat more and subsequently gain weight. There have been a few reports of abnormal bleeding and purple skin spots or very low sodium levels. In general, most people who take Paxil don't have severe enough side effects to make them want to stop taking the drug.

Food and drug interactions. There aren't any known drug reactions between Paxil and nonprescription medications, although you should discuss with your doctor any drugs you take. Paxil in combination with warfarin (Coumadin) may cause unwanted side effects. As with all the SSRIs, it should never be combined with MAOIs; if you've been taking Paxil for at least three months, you should not then take an MAOI until three weeks have passed since your last Paxil dose. Food and beverages don't affect Paxil, but you should take the medication with food or a drink if you feel nauseated.

Special concerns. Discuss with your doctor any kidney or liver disease that you have, which may affect the dosage of the Paxil you take.

Lexapro
One of the newer of the SSRIs, Lexapro was developed by isolating the medicinal component of another SSRI, Celexa (citalopram HBr). It has been prescribed for more than 12 million patients. Many patients treated with Lexapro begin to feel better within a week or two, although the full effect may take four to six weeks.

Side effects. The most common side effects include mild nausea, insomnia, sleepiness, increased sweating, fatigue, and sexual problems. All of these symptoms tend to fade away with continued treatment. In one study, only 4 percent of patients stopped taking Lexapro because of side effects. You also should be careful when combining this drug and those that affect blood clotting, such as aspirin, ibuprofen, and other nonsteroidal anti-inflammatory drugs.

Food and drug interactions. Lexapro has a low risk of interacting with other medicines in general, but you should not combine it with MAOIs or tricyclic antidepressants.

Special concerns. Discuss with your doctor any kidney or liver disease that you have, which may affect dosage.

SEROTONIN/NOREPINEPHRINE REUPTAKE INHIBITORS
This group of antidepressants is believed to affect two naturally occurring chemicals in the brain, serotonin and norepinephrine, both

of which are responsible for controlling mood and emotion. Doctors think that these chemicals may somehow improve communication among your brain cells. Experts suspect that people who are depressed have lower-than-normal levels of these chemicals; SNRIs boost these levels, which eases the depression. They include

- Effexor (venlafaxine)
- Cymbalta (duloxetine)

The most common side effects are nausea and vomiting, dizziness, insomnia, sleep problems (too much or too little, or abnormal dreams), constipation, sweating, dry mouth, tremor, gas, anxiety or agitation, vision problems (blurry vision or double vision), headache, and sexual problems.

Effexor
Approved in 1994 (a single-dose version was approved in 1997), Effexor is structurally unlike any other antidepressant. People who don't respond to the SSRIs or one of the tricyclics often do respond to Effexor. It's available in an immediate-release form taken two or three times a day, and in the extended release (XR) form it is taken once a day. This longer-acting drug can help reduce nausea.

At least one study suggests that Effexor may be more effective than Prozac in treating depression and achieving remission. Research also suggests that Effexor may help treat severe forms of PMS, in addition to treating depression.

You should take Effexor with food or milk to prevent nausea, and since dosages vary quite a bit from one patient to the next, pay very close attention to the dosage directions your doctor gives you. Your friends might take Effexor, but their dosage could be quite different from yours. Most patients begin with 75 mg in one daily dose, although some people begin with half that amount for the first week, slowly increasing to 75 mg. Dose increases are usually given in increments of 37.5 mg every four days.

Side effects. Effexor can cause nausea and drowsiness, although in general this medication is well tolerated. Other common symptoms include dry mouth, dizziness, headaches, loss of appetite, and sexual problems. Dizziness and nausea—the most common side effects—usually fade away within the first two weeks.

Less common side effects include nervousness, insomnia, and sweating. At high doses, this drug can cause a blood pressure spike or boost your heart rate. As a result, your doctor may want to monitor your blood pressure regularly, especially if you already have high blood pressure. Effexor also can raise your cholesterol level, so your doctor may ask you to have periodic cholesterol blood tests.

If you stop this medication abruptly, you can experience a discontinuation syndrome of dizziness, dry mouth, insomnia, nausea, nervousness, and sweating. Your doctor will recommend that once you've taken this drug for at least a week, you should slowly taper off the dose to minimize the risk of these symptoms. If you've been taking Effexor for more than six weeks, you should taper off the dose gradually over a two-week period.

Food and drug interactions. Discuss with your doctor any other medications you take along with Effexor; hazardous drug interactions are possible if you combine Effexor with lithium, diazepam, cimetidine, or haloperidol. You should avoid drinking alcohol with this drug. You should never combine Effexor with any MAOI because of serious and sometimes fatal reactions; make sure that you wait at least two weeks after stopping one of these two drugs before starting the other.

Special concerns. If you have liver or kidney disease, you may need lower doses of this medication; people with moderate liver disease or on kidney dialysis should cut their Effexor dosage in half.

Cymbalta

Cymbalta appears to work by helping restore the balance of serotonin and norepinephrine. Many people taking this drug begin to feel better as early as one to four weeks after starting treatment.

Side effects. The most common side effect is mild to moderate nausea that usually subsides within one to two weeks. Other common side effects include dry mouth, constipation, appetite loss, fatigue, sleepiness, and increased sweating. Because some people taking Cymbalta experience an increase in blood pressure, your doctor may periodically check your blood pressure.

Food and drug interactions. Do not mix Cymbalta with MAOIs or thioridazine (Mellaril).

Special concerns. You should not take Cymbalta if you have uncontrolled narrow-angle glaucoma.

ATYPICAL ANTIDEPRESSANTS
Atypical antidepressants include the following:

> Wellbutrin (bupropion)
> Remeron (mirtazepine)
> Serzone (nefazodone)
> Desyrel (trazodone)

Wellbutrin (Bupropion)
This newer type of antidepressant affects two other groups of naturally occurring chemicals in the brain: norepinephrine and dopamine, both of which also are responsible for controlling mood and emotion. Doctors think that these chemicals may somehow improve communication among your brain cells. Experts suspect that people who are depressed have lower-than-normal levels of these chemicals; Wellbutrin boosts these levels, which eases the depression.

This medication is available as an immediate-release pill taken three times a day; a slow release (SR) form must be taken twice a day, and an extended release (XL) form is taken once a day. Another form of this drug (Zyban) is used as an antismoking medication, not as an antidepressant. You should never take Zyban and the antidepressant form of bupropion at the same time.

Side effects. Side effects include appetite and weight loss, headache, dry mouth, skin rash, sweating, ringing in the ears, shakiness and nervousness, stomach pain, agitation, constipation, anxiety, dizziness, trouble sleeping, muscle pain, nausea and vomiting, fast heartbeat, sore throat, and frequent urination. If you have nausea, take Wellbutrin with food, and take it in the morning if you have trouble sleeping.

There's a small chance that bupropion can trigger seizures, especially if you've had seizures in the past. There's also a higher risk of seizures with this drug if you've had a head injury, a nervous system tumor, or bulimia or anorexia. Anyone with a history of seizures or eating disorders, or anyone who has suddenly stopped using alcohol or taking sedatives, should not take this drug.

Food and drug interactions. MAOIs can seriously interact with this medication. Do not take at the same time as a nicotine patch, which contains a version of the same medication; this could cause a severe blood pressure spike.

Special concerns. You should not take Wellbutrin if you have epilepsy or a seizure disorder; talk to your doctor if you have liver or kidney disease. You also should not take this drug if you have now (or have had) either bulimia or anorexia. Individuals who have abruptly stopped long-term use of alcohol or sedatives may be at risk for withdrawal.

Remeron (Mirtazapine)

Remeron represents a different approach to antidepressants. Instead of interfering with the reabsorption of certain neurotransmitters as other antidepressants do, this medication prevents neurotransmitters from binding with nerve cell receptors called alpha-2 receptors. It also stimulates the release of norepinephrine and serotonin. This increased level of norepinephrine and serotonin in the brain may improve and elevate mood. As a result, Remeron causes fewer side effects and doesn't have a harmful effect on the heart. Remeron, the only alpha-2 receptor blocker approved by the FDA specifically to treat depression, was approved in 1996 and is often helpful in treating insomnia or anxiety.

Dosages usually start at 15 mg a day, which can be increased every one or two weeks up to a maximum of 45 mg a day. You should take this drug right before bedtime, with or without food, and you should start to feel better within one to four weeks.

Side effects. Side effects include sedation and weight gain (which are much less common at higher doses), dry mouth, dizziness and lightheadedness, thirst, muscle or joint aches, constipation, increased appetite, and higher cholesterol levels. About 15 percent of patients report a spike in their cholesterol levels.

Because of a potential drug interaction, you shouldn't take mirtazapine with an MAOI. You may feel extra drowsy if you take mirtazapine with other medications or substances that also cause drowsiness, such as antihistamines, sedatives, or alcohol.

In addition, in rare circumstances, mirtazapine can cause a potentially dangerous drop in your white blood cell levels, which can increase your risk for infection. Talk to your doctor if you develop a sore throat, fever, inflammation of the mouth, flulike symptoms, or other signs of infection. Once you stop taking this drug, the condition will reverse itself. Although this condition is rare, the risk may make some doctors hesitate to prescribe it.

Food and drug interactions. If Remeron is taken with other drugs, the effects of either may be stronger, lessened, or altered in some way. It is particularly important to talk to your doctor before taking Remeron at the same time as Ativan, Valium, or Xanax.

Special concerns. If you have liver or kidney disease, you may need lower doses of this medication.

Serzone (Nefazodone)

Serzone was the first of a new type of antidepressant that combined the mechanism of an SSRI and a tricyclic; it was approved in 1994. However, its manufacturer discontinued the sale of Serzone in 2004. Serzone sales had been discontinued in 2003 in many countries because of its apparent liver toxicity, which could lead to the need for a liver transplant or even (rarely) cause death. The makers of Serzone insist that the medication was pulled because of declining sales rather than concerns about its safety, but the U.S. Food and Drug Administration warns that people who take Serzone can develop serious liver problems. Several generic formulations of nefazodone are still available in this country, however.

This drug acts on brain cells in two ways—by inhibiting the reuptake of neurotransmitters into nerve cells and by blocking nerve cell receptors. This leaves more mood-related brain chemicals available in the brain, thereby boosting mood.

Nefazodone can help people sleep, making it an obvious choice for those fighting insomnia as well as depression. This is important, since one in five people who take an SSRI also must take some type of prescription sleep aid to help them sleep.

Side effects. In rare cases, nefazodone can cause life-threatening liver failure. Side effects include dry mouth, dizziness, drowsiness, lightheadedness, nervousness, nausea, constipation, weakness, vision problems, confusion, and headache. Don't take it if you already have liver problems. Know the signs and symptoms of possible liver dysfunction, such as yellowing of your skin or the whites of your eyes, unusually dark urine, loss of appetite, nausea, or abdominal pain. Contact your doctor immediately if you experience any of these problems.

Food and drug interactions. Nefazodone significantly increases the blood levels of triazolam (Halcion) or alprazolam (Xanax), so these drugs should not be taken together. Because of its tendency to cause drowsiness, you should check with your doctor before taking it with alcohol or digoxin (Lanoxin).

Special concerns. If you have a history of mania, heart problems, or liver disease, you should discuss this with your doctor before taking nefazodone. This drug should never be used if you have a history of seizures, and it should be used cautiously if you've ever had a stroke or heart attack.

Desyrel (Trazodone)

This unusual antidepressant is unrelated to the SSRIs, MAOIs, or tricyclics and is closest in action to Serzone. It was approved in 1982. How Desyrel works is not fully understood, although researchers believe that it affects serotonin. The recommended dose is 150 mg a day, which may be increased every day by 50 mg until a final dose of 600 mg daily is reached. Once you begin to respond, your doctor may then lower the dose slowly. Because of its strong sedating properties, it is often used in combination with more energizing antidepressants to help patients sleep. Most people notice improvement after two weeks, although it may take a month before you begin to respond.

Side effects. The most common side effects are nausea, dizziness, agitation, fatigue, dry mouth, constipation, lightheadedness, headache, low blood pressure, and confusion. Painful erections have been reported, which sometimes lead to permanent impotence. You can take Desyrel with a snack to lessen dizziness and lightheadedness, unless your doctor has told you to take it on an empty stomach.

Food and drug interactions. Like other antidepressants, Desyrel should not be taken with MAOIs. You should allow at least one week after stopping the Desyrel before beginning the MAOI. The same type of interaction may occur when Desyrel is used with selegiline (Eldepryl).

Special concerns. Desyrel should be used with caution if you have heart disease, kidney disease, or liver disease. You should avoid drinking alcohol while taking Desyrel.

CYCLICS (TRICYCLICS, TETRACYCLICS, HETEROCYCLICS)

This older class of antidepressants, introduced in the 1960s, includes tricyclics and tetracyclics. It includes

> ➤ Elavil (amitriptyline)
> ➤ amoxapine

> Anafranil (clomipramine)
> Norpramin, Pertofrane (desipramine)
> Sinequan, Adapin (doxepin)
> Tofranil (imipramine)
> Ludomil (maprotiline)
> Aventyl, Pamelor (nortriptyline)
> Vivactil (protriptyline)

Although they are equally effective as the SSRIs, many physicians and patients prefer the newer drugs because the cyclics can cause annoying side effects, such as dizziness, drowsiness, dry mouth, and weight gain. Twenty years ago, if you had been depressed, your doctor would probably have started you out with a bottle of tricyclics. Today, most doctors choose a cyclic antidepressant only if a patient doesn't respond to an SSRI.

Tricyclic antidepressants (TCAs) work by interfering with the reabsorption of three brain chemicals important in mood and emotions: serotonin, norepinephrine, and dopamine. These drugs also block some cell receptors, which is why they cause so many side effects.

Side effects. Because tricyclics are less selective about which cells they affect, they typically have more side effects than other antidepressants. Side effects of TCAs include drowsiness, dry mouth, blurred vision, constipation and urinary retention, dizziness, sexual problems, increased heart rate, disorientation or confusion, headache, low blood pressure, sun sensitivity, increased appetite and weight gain, nausea, and weakness.

Maprotiline has been associated with seizures, so if you've had a history of seizures you shouldn't take this medication. Trazodone has been associated with priapism (persistent, usually painful erections not associated with sexual arousal). If this occurs, you should see a doctor right away, because many cases have required surgical correction, resulting in permanent impotence.

Tricyclics in general also are associated with a higher risk of heart attack, and they also may affect blood sugar levels. If you have diabetes, you may need to check your blood sugar more often if you take these medications. Doctors are not likely to prescribe tricyclics if you have narrow-angle glaucoma or certain types of heart disease.

Food and drug interactions. Many drugs interact with cyclics, including alcohol, illegal drugs, amphetamines, anesthetics, Aldomet, anticonvulsants, antihistamines, appetite suppressants, barbiturates, benzodiapeines, blood thinners, Catapres, Cylert, ephedrine, MAOIs, muscle relaxants, sinus medications, Tagamet, tranquilizers, and Wellbutrin.

The liquid version of doxepin (Adapin or Sinequan) should not be mixed with grape juice or carbonated beverages, since these may reduce effectiveness.

Special concerns. You should avoid stopping treatment abruptly with these medications; doing so can cause withdrawal symptoms including nausea, headache, dizziness, lethargy, and flulike symptoms. This is sometimes called discontinuation syndrome.

MONOAMINE OXIDASE INHIBITORS

These drugs are the granddaddy of antidepressant medications, first introduced in the 1950s but now much more rarely prescribed today because of a complex side effect profile. They are

➤ Nardil (phenelzine)
➤ Parnate (tranylcypromine)
➤ Marplan (isocarboxazid)
➤ Selegiline (l-Deprenyl)

Scientists believe that MAOIs relieve depression by preventing the enzyme monoamine oxidase from using the neurotransmitters norepinephrine, serotonin, and dopamine in the brain, which keeps levels of these chemicals high.

One of the major problems with this class of drugs is that anyone who takes MAOIs must follow a special restrictive diet, since these medications can interact with some foods and beverages. If you take an MAOI, you'll have to avoid a number of foods such as cheese, processed meats, and red wine, all of which contain a chemical called tyramine. MAOIs also interact with many other medications, including SSRIs, which can lead to dangerous spikes in blood pressure and other potentially life-threatening reactions.

Side effects. Because of their serious possible side effects, MAOIs are usually given only to people who don't respond to other antidepressant medications first. Side effects of MAOIs include drowsiness and fatigue; constipation or diarrhea; nausea and upset stomach; dry mouth; dizziness, lightheadedness, and low blood pressure, especially when getting up from a lying or sitting position; decreased urine; sexual problems; sleep problems; muscle twitching; weight gain and increased appetite; blurred vision; headache; restlessness, shakiness, and trembling; weakness; and sweating.

For serious side effects when mixed with certain foods, see "Food and drug interactions" below.

Food and drug interactions. MAOIs can cause dangerous interactions with certain foods, beverages, and other medications. If you take these medications, you'll face dietary restrictions that require you to limit consumption of foods that contain a high level of tyramine, such as many cheeses, pickled foods, chocolates, certain meats, beer, wine, and alcohol-free or reduced-alcohol beer and wine. The interaction of tyramine with MAOIs can cause a dangerously high increase in blood pressure, which can lead to a stroke. Your doctor can give you a complete list of dietary restrictions.

Special concerns. You should never take MAOIs with selective serotonin reuptake inhibitors (SSRIs) because of the risk of the potentially life-threatening condition serotonin syndrome. Signs and symptoms of serotonin syndrome include confusion, hallucinations, extreme agitation, fluctuations in blood pressure and heart rhythm, increased sweating, muscle rigidity, fever, seizures, and even coma. Serotonin syndrome requires immediate medical treatment.

MOOD-STABILIZING DRUGS

People with bipolar disorder are usually treated with mood stabilizers for long periods of time; if symptoms of either depression or mania appear now and then despite the mood stabilizers, additional medications may temporarily be prescribed. Mood stabilizers includes:

> ➤ lithium
> ➤ Tegretol (carbamazepine)
> ➤ Depakote (divalproex sodium)
> ➤ Zyprexa (olanzapine)
> ➤ Lamictal (lamotrigine)
> ➤ Topamax (topiramate)

Lithium

Lithium was the first drug approved to treat bipolar disorder, and it is often effective in smoothing out the emotional swings of mania and easing the lows of chronic recurring depression. Lithium can quickly reverse mania in 80 percent of people and stabilize mood in 60 to 70 percent. While it can ease depression, it is particularly effective in calming mania. Some patients who take lithium to control mania but who are still depressed are prescribed a second antidepressant to control their depression.

Although scientists aren't exactly sure why lithium works, some believe it may normalize certain brain chemicals (serotonin and norepinephrine) that are linked to emotions and behavior. Unfortunately, it's not a miracle cure for everyone—symptoms will totally disappear only for 20 percent of people with manic depression; the rest have varying rates of success. And for some people, lithium simply stops working.

Side effects. Thirst and frequent urination are two of the most common, least serious side effects; some people also gain weight in the first few months of taking this drug. People with either psoriasis or diabetes may notice that the condition worsens during lithium treatment.

Contact your doctor at the very first sign of toxicity: sleepiness, sluggishness, unsteadiness, tremors and muscle twitches, vomiting or diarrhea.

Food and drug interactions. When taking lithium, you should never restrict your salt intake; too little salt could increase lithium's effects. Avoid drinking too much tea or coffee, which increases the risk of adverse effects. Drink at least 8 to 12 glasses of water a day, avoid alcohol, and don't skip meals.

Special concerns. There's a very thin line between what's an effective therapeutic dose of lithium and what is toxic with this medication. For this reason, your doctor will want to measure the level of lithium in your blood from time to time to make sure you're not getting too much.

Mood-Stabilizing Anticonvulsants

If lithium isn't working, the second-generation mood stabilizers that a doctor may select are the anticonvulsants Tegretol or Depakote, which are widely used as alternatives. These medications can be especially helpful for difficult-to-treat bipolar episodes.

In addition, third-generation anticonvulsants (Lamictal and Topamax) can sometimes effectively treat bipolar disorder that has not responded to other medications. Because studies have suggested that people with bipolar disorder are at risk of becoming manic or developing rapid cycling during treatment with antidepressants, mood-stabilizing medications generally are required, alone or in combination with antidepressants, to protect people with bipolar disorder from this.

Side effects. The most potentially serious side effect is with Lamictal (lamotrigine), which may cause a rash ranging in severity from mild sunburn to a fatal condition. If taking this drug, report all rashes to your doctor. Rarely, Lamictal causes agitation, anxiety, concentration problems, confusion, irritability, and mania.

Topamax (topiramate) may cause slowed movements, memory problems, fatigue, confusion, and sleepiness. Rarely, it may cause sedation, anxiety, and confusion.

Food and drug interactions. Avoid taking these drugs with Dilantin (phenytoin), alcohol, phenobarbital, or primidone. Combining Topamax (topiramate) and lamotrigine with Depakote or Tegretol may alter the concentrations of the drugs. When taken with topiramate, Depakote or Tegretol can lower the concentration of topiramate in the blood. Topiramate has no effect on the blood levels of Tegretol, but it can lower the concentration of Depakote. Patients taking Tegretol and lamotrigine together may have slightly lower blood levels of lamotrigine; Depakote can double the blood levels of lamotrigine.

Special concerns. Because there is some evidence that Depakote may lead to hormone changes in teenage girls and polycystic ovary syndrome in women who begin taking the medication before age 20, a doctor should carefully monitor young girls taking Depakote.

Zyprexa (Olanzapine)

This schizophrenia drug is the newest medication to be approved for the short-term treatment of acute manic episodes. Research suggests that it may better control symptoms than Depakote. Unlike lithium, Zyprexa doesn't require blood tests. Research suggests that Zyprexa can help manage manic episodes by stabilizing mood.

Side effects. Zyprexa (olanzapine) may cause sleepiness, dry mouth, weakness, dizziness, and weight gain. Life-threatening pancreatitis (inflammation of the pancreas) has occurred, according to the U.S. Food and Drug Administration, in some adults and children.

Food and drug interactions. None

Special considerations. None

WHAT YOU NEED TO KNOW

- ▶ Most experts believe that you become depressed when the levels of chemical neurotransmitters drop too low, so that messages can't cross the gaps between your brain cells and communication in your brain slows down.
- ▶ Neurotransmitters most related to depression are serotonin, norepinephrine, and dopamine; antidepressants raise the levels of these chemicals, thereby easing depression.
- ▶ It's very important to take medication exactly as prescribed for it to work.
- ▶ There are several types of antidepressants: selective serotonin reuptake inhibitors (SSRIs), serotonin norepinephrine reuptake inhibitors (SNRIs), chemically unrelated miscellaneous antidepressants, tricyclics, and monoamine oxidase inhibitors (MAOIs).
- ▶ Each type of antidepressant has different side effects, but in general the newer SSRIs and SNRIs have fewer side effects and are less dangerous in overdose than the tricyclics and MAOIs.
- ▶ The FDA in 2004 warned that antidepressants may increase suicidal thoughts and suicide attempts in a small number of children and adolescents, and it required manufacturers to include labels with strong warnings on their products.
- ▶ If you're taking an antidepressant and you start thinking about suicide or you suddenly feel agitated, restless, and irritable, you should tell your parents and contact your doctor immediately.
- ▶ SSRIs are the most popular antidepressants available; they include Prozac, Paxil, Zoloft, Luvox, Celexa, and Lexapro.
- ▶ Serotonin/norepinephrine reuptake inhibitors (SNRIs) include Effexor (venlafaxine) and Cymbalta (duloxetine).
- ▶ Atypical antidepressants include Wellbutrin (bupropion), Remeron (mirtazepine), Serzone (nefazodone), and Desyrel (trazodone).
- ▶ The cyclics (tricyclics, tetracyclics, heterocyclics) include Elavil (amitriptyline), amoxapine, Anafranil (clomipramine), Norpramin, Pertofrane (desipramine), Sinequan, Adapin (doxepin), Tofranil (imipramine), Ludomil (maprotiline), Aventyl or Pamelor (nortriptyline), and Vivactil (protriptyline).
- ▶ Monoamine oxidase inhibitors (MAOIs) include Nardil (phenelzine), Parnate (tranylcypromine), and Marplan (isocarboxazid).

➤ Mood-stabilizing medications taken to treat bipolar disorder include lithium, Tegretol, Depakote, Zyprexa (olanzapine), Lamictal (lamotrigine), and Topamax (topiramate).

7

Helping Yourself with Depression

If you're depressed, working with a therapist and taking medication are two of the best things you can do to start feeling better. However, there are plenty of other things you can do on your own that may help you feel better, too. Most of these alternative treatments have been found effective to some degree in helping teens fight depression. They may seem simple, but evidence strongly suggests that they can have an impact. For example, research is quite clear that getting exercise when you're feeling depressed can really help perk up your mood. So can eating right, getting enough of sleep, and practicing some type of relaxation method, such as yoga or meditation.

WORK IT OUT!

Jumping on your bike or lacing up your Nikes is probably the very last thing you really feel like doing if you're truly depressed. Many teens who are clinically depressed feel so lethargic they can scarcely find the strength to climb out of bed and somehow get through the day. Yet there's fairly good evidence showing that exercise can improve your mood if you have mild to moderate depression (and it certainly won't do any harm). By stimulating the production of neurochemicals in the brain—the same chemicals targeted by antidepressants—exercise can help lift you out of a depressive mood. Exercise also improves circulation and increases blood flow and oxygen to the brain.

One recent research study at Duke University Medical Center that looked at the value of exercise training in older patients with major depressive disorders concluded that although antidepressants improved symptoms more quickly at first, after 16 weeks of treatment exercise was just as effective in reducing depression. Other studies show that jogging for 30 minutes three times a week can be as effective as psychotherapy in treating depression (any exercise is fine, but the more energetic and aerobic, the better). In a 2000 study at Duke University, researchers discovered that exercise works at least as well as the popular antidepressant Zoloft in treating clinical depression and keeping the condition from returning.

Some people say that when they exercise, they can think more clearly and feel better about themselves afterward. (They're also probably losing weight and getting stronger, which helps them enjoy a sense of well-being.) After exercise, many people report that they sleep better and feel less nervous, anxious, and negative. And studies suggest that when participants continue to exercise, the ongoing improvement is even greater.

You can expect your mood to improve just 10 minutes after you start exercising, and studies suggest that it should continue to get better for up to 20 minutes. Once you continue to exercise, the ongoing improvements are even better, and they last for months. Researchers conclude that although medication may work more quickly to ease depression, exercise provides more long-term benefits.

What kind of exercise? If you have any health issues, consult your doctor before starting an exercise program and ask him or her to recommend one that will be practical, safe, and healthy. Walking is one of the best exercises for helping depression, but just about any aerobic exercise is effective. You don't need any special equipment except a good pair of walking shoes. It's free, you don't have to compete with anybody else, and you can do it anytime, anywhere. You can walk on the track at your local school after hours, along rural walking trails or abandoned roads, or at the mall. You don't need any special clothes to walk, either. Whatever you happen to be wearing at the time will be just fine. And it's pretty safe, too—you probably won't suffer from any overuse injuries that you might have with other types of exercise.

If walking seems too tame for you, try another form of aerobic exercise (exercise that boosts your breathing and heart rate): biking, jogging, swimming, and sporting activities such as racquetball, weight lifting, sprinting, softball, and football. Self-defense methods such as tae kwon do can help improve depression, too. In one study, tae kwon do participants were more vigorous and less anxious, depressed, angry, tired, and confused after only one 75-minute session.

Yoga also has been found to improve depression. In a yoga class, you learn a range of meditation practices including breathing techniques that exercise your lungs and calm your nervous system.

Choose something you enjoy. If you want to stick with it, it's important to pick an activity that you might enjoy—even if it's something as basic as walking around the block. If you do it as often as you can (three to four times a week is ideal) you may be surprised at how much better it can make you feel. Some people enjoy the routine of doing the exact same exercise every time. Others like more variety and spend part of their exercise period doing one kind of exercise and part of the time doing another. You might shoot some hoops in your driveway and then go for a walk or a bike ride. This can make exercise more interesting.

Any form of regular exercise can boost your mood. If you loathe rowing machines or can't stand exercise videos, it doesn't make much sense to inflict that type of exercise on yourself. If you love your dog, then make a pact to take him for a walk every day. If swimming has always been your favorite sport, then try that. The key is to choose something you can reasonably expect to be able to do at least three times a week.

If you like team sports, sign up with your local softball league or go out for a new sport at school. If you're more the solitary sort, consider swimming, hiking, dancing, skating, outdoor chores, walking, or yoga. If you have an exercise bike or a treadmill at home (maybe one of your parents is an exercise buff), some kids find they don't mind exercising if they can watch a movie or listen to music while exercising.

Make it a part of your life. Try to start thinking about integrating exercise into your everyday life. For instance, if you usually take the escalator at the mall, instead try walking up those stairs. If you're running errands, park farther away and walk the extra blocks. If you're already walking your dog, add just 10 minutes to the routine. If you're biking, try riding 10 or 20 minutes longer.

Find a buddy. Since you're probably not very motivated to get moving, it can help if you have an exercise buddy or if you join a gym or a structured program. A health club or gym is a great place for people who enjoy exercising with others in an atmosphere that is pleasant and sociable.

Set a schedule. If you've been so depressed you can't get out of bed, or if you've been parking yourself in front of the TV or the computer because you've been too depressed to do anything else, even 15 minutes working on deep breathing exercises could be called exercise.

Remember that exercise doesn't mean you have to train for a marathon—just tell yourself that you'll get dressed and walk around the block. Then promise to walk around the block at least three times that day. The next day, do more. Try to improve just a little bit each day—but if you can't, don't beat yourself up. You might not be able to handle a lot of exercise, so try to feel good about what you can do. The point is to do something, no matter what. Even if you don't enjoy it today, eventually you will.

As you start to feel better, you can boost your exercise level from a walk around the block to a bike ride down the street and then perhaps a group aerobics class. The important thing is to start slowly and gradually increase the time you spend exercising, until you're exercising three days a week for 30 minutes a time. At first you may want to exercise for just 10 minutes, then 15, and then 20. You should keep increasing your exercise periods until you reach your goal.

One of the hardest things about exercise for most people is to find the time. Between school, homework, after-school jobs, sports, music practice, babysitting—it may seem as if you just don't have time for exercise. If you're worrying while you're exercising, it won't be much fun and you probably won't enjoy it.

Once you start, try to maintain a regular schedule of exercise. Many kids find that every other day (Monday, Wednesday, and Friday) makes a good program. Some kids make a list of exercise options and then choose from the list each day. If it's raining, you can hop on the exercise bike while watching a DVD. If the softball team doesn't have a game, you can go for a swim instead.

Watch out for . . . If you feel any pain or experience anything other than the normal sensation of muscle fatigue, stop exercising at once. If you're not used to moving around very much, the first few times you should ice right after exercising and then take a warm bath to relieve those aches and pains that come when you inadvertently overexercise. Always work out at your own pace—you're not trying out for the Olympics. If you're sick or have a fever, skip exercise. As you exercise, you can gradually begin to increase the difficulty of your workouts. But go slowly. Don't suddenly add 20 pounds to your weights or go from running a half mile to five miles. Your body adapts better to slow change, and you'll be able to avoid all those aches and pains that come with too much exercise before your body is ready for it.

Don't get caught in the "not yet" trap, putting off exercise until you have enough money to buy the expensive jogging shoes or trendy equipment, or until the weather's better, or until you're feeling less depressed. Most exercise doesn't take special clothing or equipment— just a little willpower.

Make it playtime. If you want to stick with your exercise plan, tell yourself it's playtime, not work. Ask your friends to exercise with you and reward yourself each time you exercise or after you've exercised for a week. Try contributing a dollar to a jar each day you exercise, to use for something you've been wanting. Or maybe your mom or dad would contribute the dollar for you as an added incentive. After exercising becomes so much a part of your life that you don't even think about it, you'll no longer need to reward yourself.

Some kids find it hard to get motivated to exercise during the pouring rain or when it's freezing outside, which is why an indoor option such as an exercise bike or rowing machine works well. You don't have to plunk down your entire month's allowance, however. People are always selling their machines when their intentions never quite make it to reality. You can often find these at flea markets, in the classified section of the newspaper, at secondhand stores, or at local swap shops.

Above all, don't fall into the "all or nothing" rut: "I missed my exercise today. There's no point in continuing." Other kids fall into the mistaken idea that if they don't run 20 miles every day, there's no point in running at all. Avoid sabotaging yourself. Missing one day doesn't mean you can't simply pick up where you left off tomorrow. And running one mile, or a half mile, or even half a block is always better than not running at all.

If you miss a day, several days, or even weeks of exercise, don't give up and stop exercising. Just start again. If you have a long hiatus or have stopped exercising because of an injury or illness, start again gradually.

MANAGE YOUR STRESS

Stress management may sound like something corporate executives worry about, but as any kid can testify, if you're depressed you probably are also dealing with a lot of stress. Between the educational pressures of school, teachers, homework, tests and quizzes; the pressure to get into college; and the social pressures of boyfriends and girlfriends, being accepted or rejected, and getting asked to the right parties or the prom, kids probably have more stress per square inch than any business executive. In fact, stress and depression can affect each other, so methods designed to reduce stress will also help ease depression.

Relaxation Training

Relaxation training or meditation may help you keep calm and may enhance the effects of psychotherapy. Learning how to relax is a crucial part of stress management, because when you can relax your body you'll automatically reduce the harmful effects of stress.

When you hear the word *relax*, you may think it means plopping down on the sofa to watch your favorite reality TV show or sitting in a hammock with a good book. That's certainly one way to relax. But in this case, "relaxing" is a very deliberate attempt to unclench your tensed-up muscles while refocusing your thoughts on peaceful things. As you practice this type of relaxation, you'll notice that your breathing slows down; at the same time, your blood pressure drops and your muscles relax.

Muscle relaxation. Here are some basic tips on how to relax your muscles, which can help you feel less stress. First, you'll need to find a position that feels comfortable—you can either sit or lie down.

1. Close your eyes.
2. Take slow, deep breaths.
3. As you mentally hear the word *relax*, consciously relax the very top of your head. When you feel the top of your head relax, move down to the eye area, relaxing those muscles. Move on to the sinus area of your face.
4. Repeat the word *relax* as you consciously relax each muscle group. Don't move on until you can feel that area relax.
5. Move on to your ears and the back of your neck. This is the area that holds a lot of tension, so don't rush. Don't mentally move on until you can feel those muscles relax.
6. Move slowly down your body, all the way to your toes, relaxing muscles as you go. Go slowly, and wait for the muscle to relax before moving to the next area.
7. Once you've relaxed your entire body, simply enjoy the feeling of total ease for about 10 minutes, at least. Allow yourself to drift along and experience this new sensation.

Some kids have trouble mentally willing a muscle to relax. If you're having a problem with this, try progressive muscle relaxation. What you'll be doing here is purposely tensing just one set of muscles while letting the rest of the body relax. This may sound easy, but it might take a bit of practice. The tendency is to tense up a whole bunch of muscles at the same time. If you have trouble tightening and relaxing muscles, practice first with your fist to get the hang of it. Clench your fist tightly and then relax it. That's what you should be doing with each of the muscle groups in your body in this exercise.

1. Sit or lie down and close your eyes.
2. Begin taking slow, deep breaths.
3. Start with the muscles behind your neck. Firmly tense just those muscles, keeping the rest of your body relaxed.
4. Hold for five seconds and then relax those muscles— visualize those muscles relaxing.
5. Now move on to the muscles of your shoulders. Tense those muscles, keeping the rest of your muscles relaxed. Tighten the muscles as much as possible, hold for five seconds, and then relax.

Breathing. While it's important to know how to relax your muscles, there's another important body function you need to control if you're going to relax—your breathing. If you can learn to control your breathing, you can learn how to relax.

You probably think you know all there is about breathing—it's just a matter of inhaling and exhaling, right? But in fact, when you get tense, your breathing becomes more shallow as you use your chest muscles to breathe in, so that only the top part of your lungs fill with air. As you take quick, shallow breaths, your oxygen level falls and stress chemicals pour into your bloodstream. The more stress

Be Careful!

If you have an injury or a weak muscle group, be careful when tensing that area. You might want to skip it altogether.

chemicals, the more stress you feel. And the more stress you feel, the faster you breathe, which lowers your oxygen level even more. It's a vicious circle.

What you need to do is to learn how to breathe the way singers do, from your diaphragm (a muscle at the bottom of your lungs that helps you breathe). Now you're ready to learn how to begin relaxation breathing. First, find a comfortable position, either sitting or lying down.

1. Close your eyes.
2. Place your hands on your lap and relax your arms.
3. Take slow, deep breaths.
4. Breathe rhythmically from your diaphragm, not your chest.

Here are a few other deep breathing exercises that can help you control stress:

Stress-Busting One to Four
1. Close your eyes, place your hands on your lap, and relax your arms.
2. Inhale, counting very slowly from one to four.
3. Exhale, counting slowly back down.
4. Do this for several breaths.

Stress-Busting Countdown
1. Close your eyes, place your hands on your lap, and relax your arms.
2. Inhale, and say "10."
3. Exhale.
4. As you inhale again, say "nine."
5. Exhale.
6. Keep counting down with each breath in (if you start to get dizzy, slow down).
7. When you get to "zero" you should feel very calm.

You probably won't be able to breathe like this constantly, but it's a good technique to use when you're feeling stressed, tense, or upset. It's even possible to prevent some kinds of anxiety by practicing deep, controlled breathing before a stressful situation.

You won't go into an altered state of consciousness just by deep breathing, and you won't be hypnotized. But you'll help distract yourself from your worries and anxiety and may give yourself an energy

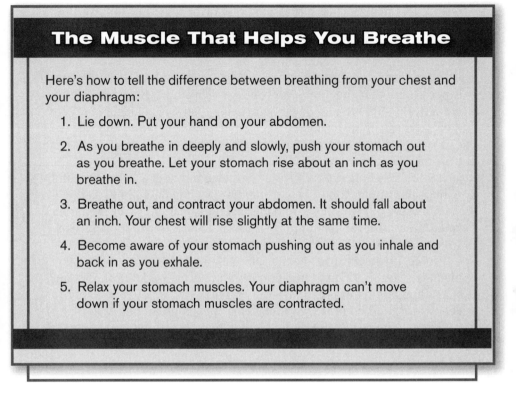

The Muscle That Helps You Breathe

Here's how to tell the difference between breathing from your chest and your diaphragm:

1. Lie down. Put your hand on your abdomen.

2. As you breathe in deeply and slowly, push your stomach out as you breathe. Let your stomach rise about an inch as you breathe in.

3. Breathe out, and contract your abdomen. It should fall about an inch. Your chest will rise slightly at the same time.

4. Become aware of your stomach pushing out as you inhale and back in as you exhale.

5. Relax your stomach muscles. Your diaphragm can't move down if your stomach muscles are contracted.

boost, which can be critical to those who are depressed. You can practice your deep breathing almost anytime—as you drive to school, during sports, or before you have to get up in front of the class and give a talk.

Meditation. Meditation techniques have been refined over the years in many cultures and by people around the world. Rooted in the traditions of some of the world's great religions, meditation is an effective alternative tool for relaxation and stress reduction.

Although people around the world have been meditating for centuries, only during the past 30 years have scientists begun to focus on the physical effects of meditation on human health. During the 1960s Americans were intrigued by tales of Eastern yogis and masters who could perform extraordinary feats of physical control during altered states of consciousness. Western scientists began to study the possibility of voluntary control over the autonomic nervous system, just as new technology allowed them to substantiate some of these reports at medical research institutes. Using biofeedback machines, researchers realized that it was possible for people to physically slow their heart rate and lower their blood pressure simply by meditating. More scientists began to realize that meditation might be a valuable nonmedicinal tool to reduce stress.

Many teens say that their lives are packed so full of activities and expectations that they have no time for relaxation. Between school, homework, athletics, and extracurricular activities, kids today say they have no time to spend in silent contemplation. Many are so caught up in planning for the future that there's not much time left over for pleasure in the here and now.

If you're feeling stress, meditating twice a day can help you calm down. The more you practice meditation, the less time you will need to spend on it, but it remains useful in calming and preparing you. Allow at least 10 minutes—ideally 20—for meditation in each session.

People often confuse meditation with concentration. When you meditate, you're trying to quiet your mind and slow down those constant thoughts naturally, by deeply relaxing your body and trying to keep your mind completely blank. That means no thoughts at all.

To meditate, you'll begin with your deep breathing and then try one of the relaxation methods described above. Once you're relaxed, here's all you do:

1. As you breathe out, silently repeat a word or a phrase (such as "om" or "calm").
2. If a thought pops into your head—and you'll be surprised how often this happens —calmly let it drift away. Don't get worked up about it.
3. Return to your meditation word.
4. Continue for 10 or 15 minutes. Once you get good at meditating, you can lengthen the period.

DIET: YOU FEEL WHAT YOU EAT

People have been talking about the value of a healthy diet as a depression treatment since the 1950s. Although there's still not much evidence to support the use of diet therapy for people with depression, nutrients are required for proper brain function.

Many experts recommend eating a healthy diet high in complex carbohydrates and protein, avoiding simple sugars (sweets, pies, cakes, cookies, candy, soda) that can cause fluctuating blood sugar levels and emotional ups and downs. It may also be a good idea to stay away from food with a lot of chemical additives or preservatives that may trigger ups and downs for chemically sensitive individuals, although this is more controversial. Some research has shown that people who are depressed tend to have low levels of folic acid, a vitamin found most abundantly in leafy green vegetables.

The fact is, few people eat a truly healthy diet, and teens—having a penchant for fast food, pizza, junk food, and soda—are at special risk. Since the diet of most people lacks key nutrients, you may want to look at the kind of food you're eating to see where you can improve. Eat healthy foods low in sugars and fats, such as fruits and vegetables. Diet therapy suggests a diet balanced in nutrients and vitamins, which are essential for normal functioning of the body. Vitamin B_1, for instance, is essential for energy production and nerve cell function. Vitamin B_6 is important in maintaining hormone balance, Vitamin C increases immune system functions in general, and many other suggested foods such as bitter greens and endives help cleanse the liver and improve digestion.

Omega-3 fatty acids are also thought to be necessary to healthy mental functioning. Essential fatty acids are necessary to the human diet, yet we can't produce our own. Instead, we must obtain these essential fatty acids in the foods we consume.

Vitamin B appears to help relieve stress. If you take supplemental B complex with your regular multivitamin and mineral, you should take a combination with extra C; this helps your body metabolize the B vitamins better.

WRITE IT DOWN

Darlene had been abused by her father when she was a middle school student. When she entered therapy a few years later, she found it extremely difficult to discuss the abuse with her therapist. At his suggestion, she began to write down her feelings about the abuse in a journal; at each session, she'd let her therapist read what she'd written as a way of moving the therapy process along.

Many therapists, just like Darlene's psychologist, have found that journaling can help people who are depressed feel better. In fact, a few studies have found that certain kinds of written records help combat depression. Writing in a journal or notebook or on a computer can help you think about and plan what to do about problems. As you actively work on thinking about your problems and how you can change them, you may notice that you're feeling less depressed and more satisfied.

Many teens are already avid journalers. If you like to write or you keep an online journal or blog, write a few sentences that describe what you've been doing and how you felt. You also should write about your everyday feelings. Writing this all down can help you sort everything out and experience the feelings without keeping them inside you.

You're writing for yourself—you don't have to show this to your parents or your therapist. It's just a way to clear out negative thoughts and help you clarify how you do feel about things. You're not going to be graded and you don't have to produce an award-winning essay. What's important is that you write as often as possible about how you feel and what you are thinking.

As you're writing about your feelings, here's something else to try. Keep a "happiness journal" and start by making a list of the experiences you've had when you've been happy or when you had a very good time. Describe these special moments: Perhaps you visited a beautiful canyon or mountain scene, or maybe you just had a great time with your friends.

Another day, make a list of the things you like about yourself. Maybe you like your sense of fair play, or maybe you're a great guitar player. Maybe it's something small, such as how well you get along with your friends.

On another day, make a list of things you're thankful for—it doesn't have to be major. Perhaps you're thankful for your kitten or the fact you got the good teacher for English class.

Finally, keep a running collection of inspiring quotes, poems, prayers, or affirmations. Affirmations are inspiring statements you can repeat throughout the day as a way of self-improvement: "I'm completely calm and at ease in social situations." Reread this "happiness journal" regularly to help keep your mind focused on good, rather than negative, things.

Keep adding new items to your journal as you think of them, rereading them regularly to help keep your mind focused on good things instead of negative images.

HELPING YOURSELF

You'll get better faster if you take an active role in your treatment. Remember, you're not just a patient waiting for the doctor to fix your problems—you and your therapist must work as a team. Of course, people who are depressed often don't feel much like taking control of anything, and from where you're sitting now, you may well have serious doubts about whether your medication or your therapy will work. That's your depression talking; depression can make you feel hopeless, powerless, and incapable. By taking charge of your treatment, you're taking the first step toward getting back control of your life.

Hang in there. Your doctor has probably already explained that you won't feel better right away after starting an antidepressant. It just doesn't work that fast, and if you're hoping it will, you're bound to be disappointed. It may take as long as four to six weeks to work, and sometimes the first medication you try won't work at all. Don't give up. You may need to try one or two or even three prescriptions before finding just the right one that works for you.

Psychotherapy can take a while to help, too. You may have been depressed for months or years, so you can't expect to change the way you think and automatically react to situations overnight. But research studies are clear: If you give them time, these treatments will almost certainly help. Almost everybody who is depressed improves with medication and therapy.

You may feel that things are hopeless and that they're never going to get any better—those feelings are just symptoms of your depression. If you give yourself some time to allow your treatment to work, you'll feel better again.

Work with your therapist. Opening up to a therapist isn't easy, and some kids worry that the therapist may reveal their secrets to their parents. But if you can't be honest with your therapist and you can't trust that person, therapy won't help you as much. You should make sure to talk about the issue of confidentiality right from the beginning. That's the time to ask your therapist exactly how much confidentiality you can expect, how detailed the reports to parents will be, and what the limits are.

If you have doubts about how therapy is going, or you're not sure about your therapist's approach, don't keep it to yourself. Remember, your parents are paying this therapist to listen to you—so talk openly with your therapist about your feelings. He or she will be happy to have your feedback. Together, you might be able to work out a new approach that works better.

Be flexible. Your therapist may have suggestions that you've never thought about before. He or she may push you to do something that feels uncomfortable. Even if you're not sure, try to keep an open mind and at least listen to what the therapist is saying.

Take your medicine correctly. Take your medicine exactly the way your physician prescribes it, at the same time every day. It's easier to remember if you do it along with another activity, such as brushing your teeth, eating breakfast, or getting into bed. If you use a weekly pillbox, it will be easier to see if you've missed a dose.

Above all, never stop taking your medicine without your doctor's permission. If you're having uncomfortable side effects and you want to stop taking your antidepressant, talk to your doctor. You'll probably need to reduce your dose gradually. If you stop suddenly, you may have side effects, or the abrupt change may cause your depression to return. Many teenagers start to feel better when they've been taking their antidepressants and figure it's time to stop. In fact, many people need to keep taking antidepressants even when they're feeling well to prevent a relapse. If you're feeling good now, that could be because your medicine is working.

Avoid drugs and alcohol. This may seem obvious, but a lot of depressed people—especially teenagers—also have problems with alcohol or other drugs. Sometimes the depression comes first and kids start using drugs or drinking as a way to forget about their problems or sad feelings. Other kids start experimenting with alcohol or drugs and then develop depression as a result of the drug itself or withdrawal from it. Sometimes it's hard to tell which came first.

The most important point is that if you're depressed and you're also using drugs or alcohol, the sooner you get treatment, the better. Either problem can make the other worse and lead to bigger trouble, such as flunking out of school, drunk driving, or stealing to get money for drugs. You need to be honest about both problems—first with yourself and then with someone who can help you get into treatment. It's the only way to get better and stay better.

The Alcohol Trap

Although some people use alcohol as an escape from depression, it can lead to vitamin deficiencies that can make you feel worse.

HERBAL TREATMENTS

In addition to antidepressant medications, some people turn to herbal treatments to ease their depression. The best-known treatment is an herb called St. John's wort, which is grown as a decorative plant but is also available in tablets, tea, tincture, decoction, oil, and capsules at natural health food stores, grocery stores, and drug stores.

There is some scientific evidence that supports the idea that this plant extract (Hypericum perforatum) is useful. An overview of 23 European clinical studies found that the herb might be useful in cases of mild to moderate depression. The studies, which included 1,757 outpatients, reported that St. John's wort was more effective than a placebo (a "dummy" pill designed to have no effect) and had fewer side effects than some standard antidepressants. However, a more recent study by the drug company Pfizer suggests that St. John's wort is of no benefit in treating major depression of moderate severity. Another study by the National Institutes of Health, the Office of Dietary Supplements, and the National Institute of Mental Health found that St. John's wort was no more effective for treating major depression of moderate severity than placebo.

So what does all this research mean to you? Most doctors would say that in mild cases of depression it may help, and in most cases won't hurt to try. However, do not take St. John's wort on your own without telling your therapist—and never combine it with antidepressants. In addition, St. John's wort interacts with certain drugs, including certain drugs used to control HIV infection (such as indinavir). Other research shows that St. John's wort can interact with chemotherapy drugs, anesthesia drugs, and drugs that help prevent the body from rejecting transplanted organs (such as cyclosporine). Using St. John's wort limits these drugs' effectiveness. That's why it's important to tell all of your doctors about any therapy that you're considering, including any dietary supplements.

Some patients turn to St. John's wort because antidepressant drugs don't help their symptoms or because they experience unpleasant side effects from their prescription medication. Others cannot afford their medication, and use St. John's wort because it costs less than many antidepressant medications and is sold without a prescription. In Europe, St. John's wort is widely prescribed for depression, and it remains among the top-selling herbal products in the United States.

Remember that herbal products such as St. John's wort are considered dietary supplements by the U.S. Food and Drug Administration, and the rules governing these products are less strict than those for medications. Herbal products can be sold without requiring studies on dosage, safety, or effectiveness. In addition, because the rules governing dietary supplements are not as strict, the strength and quality of herbal products are often unpredictable. Products can differ in content not only from brand to brand but from batch to batch, and label details may be misleading or inaccurate.

WHAT YOU NEED TO KNOW

> There are some things you can do on your own to treat your depression, including getting plenty of exercise, eating right, getting the right amount of sleep, keeping a journal, and practicing some type of relaxation method, such as yoga or meditation.

> People who are depressed get better faster if they take an active role in their treatment.

> In addition to antidepressant medications, some people turn to herbal treatments to ease their depression. The best-known treatment is an herb called St. John's wort.

8

Breaking the Cycle:
Depression and Other Issues

Depression can be a serious mental health issue all by itself, but it's also a common by-product of other mental health prob- lems, including anxiety and panic, obesity, cutting and self-abuse, and post-traumatic stress disorder.

ANXIETY AND PANIC

Karin has suffered severe panic attacks that make her feel as if she's having a heart attack or going crazy, for no apparent reason. Her panic attacks have occurred while she was at the mall shopping, and as a result she's afraid to go back to the mall for fear that it might trigger another attack. Yet all of her friends love to go shopping and regularly meet at the mall every Friday night. Karin became increas- ingly depressed as she felt isolated and alone, listening to her friends talk and laugh about all the fun they'd had. She began to worry that soon her friends would exclude her and she'd have no friends to turn to—yet the idea of going back to the mall was intolerable. Soon Karin was so depressed at the way her panic attacks were affecting her life that she could barely drag herself to school.

As you can see from Karin's case, many mental health problems can trigger depression when the reality of the disorder's effects becomes apparent. Soon you're dealing not just with one problem but with two.

If you're like Karin and you struggle with anxiety or panic attacks, you may be very aware of the symptoms, which include heart palpitations, chest pain or discomfort, sweating, trembling, tingling sensations, feelings of choking, fear of dying or losing control, and feelings of unreality. You may also find yourself, like Karin, trapped in a vicious cycle of symptoms and panic, panic and more symptoms. Add to this the feeling of depression, and your situation may seem unbearable.

Affecting twice as many girls as boys, panic disorder typically starts during late adolescence, and the risk of developing the condition may be inherited. In the worst-case scenario, people get so worried about experiencing a panic attack that they avoid any situation in which they would feel helpless if a panic attack were to occur. When your life becomes so restricted that you don't want to leave the house for fear of having an attack (as occurs about one-third of the time), the condition is called agoraphobia. Agoraphobia develops as a result of the fear of another panic attack, not from fear of an object or event. Early treatment of panic disorder can often prevent agoraphobia from developing.

Several factors can play a role in the development of anxiety conditions such as panic disorder. There seems to be a connection between the development of a panic disorder and a significant loss or major transition, such as moving, going to a new school, or graduating. In addition, the disorder may be influenced by genetics; studies with twins have confirmed the possibility of inheriting panic disorder. Brain malfunctions also may influence the development of panic disorder, although a specific brain problem has not yet been identified.

The symptoms of panic themselves, however, are caused by the overactivity of the body's normal fear response. The symptoms that you feel during a panic attack are typical of your body's normal "flight or fight" response that anyone would experience in a life-or-death situation. If a mountain lion suddenly appeared out of the bushes in your backyard, it's likely that your heart would start to pound, your stomach would knot, and you'd start breathing more quickly as your body prepared itself to fight or to run away from danger. If you were facing a large predator, those symptoms would make perfect sense.

Your body's fight-or-flight response becomes a problem when it kicks in when there isn't a life-or-death situation. During a panic attack, these symptoms appear out of the blue, in apparently harmless situations such as shopping, taking a walk, or even sleeping.

Life experiences and learned behavior also play a part in the development of a panic disorder. Although the first panic attacks may come out of the blue, eventually you help trigger them yourself by responding to physical symptoms of an attack. Let's say you have panic disorder and your heart starts to pound after you've run a few laps around the ball field in gym class. If you interpret your racing heartbeat as a symptom of an attack, the anxiety you feel when you experience the racing heartbeats can trigger a real panic attack. Of course, sometimes exercise (along with certain medications, coffee, and so on) may itself cause a panic attack. It can be hard to tell the difference, which is why thorough treatment by a mental health professional is so important.

Treatment. A mental health professional can diagnose panic and anxiety disorders, as well as depression. If you've been diagnosed with an anxiety or panic disorder and depression, you'll be glad to hear that these conditions respond in most cases to a combination of medication and carefully targeted psychotherapy. It's important to get treatment, however, because if you don't, these disorders can eventually get in the way of your life.

The first step in treatment is simply to learn as much as you can about panic disorder, and the health expert you visit will help explain the problem to you. Simply learning that you're not crazy and you're not going to have a heart attack can be very reassuring.

Depression and anxiety or panic are usually treated with a combination of antidepressants (see Chapter 6) and cognitive-behavioral therapy (CBT) (see Chapter 5). Medication can help you get your depression under control, and CBT can help you focus on changing your thinking in a process called cognitive restructuring. With this method, you'll learn how to replace the panicky automatic thought you have ("I'm going to die!") with more realistic thoughts ("This will only last a few minutes"). To eliminate those automatic thoughts, you'll figure out the core beliefs underlying these thoughts—and then change those beliefs. Of course, changing the way you think isn't easy; it can mean undoing years of automatic thought patterns. Truly reprogramming what you think about yourself ("I'm incompetent") isn't as easy as it might seem.

The behavioral part of CBT focuses on changing your reactions to anxiety-provoking situations and handling the stress that arises during these situations. If you have panic disorder, your therapist might help you focus on exposing yourself to the physical sensations you feel during a panic attack. People with panic disorder are more afraid of the actual attack than they are of specific objects or events.

During your treatment, your therapist will probably assign "homework"—specific problems that you'll need to work on between sessions. Exposure will be carried out only when you're ready and will be done gradually and with your permission. You'll work with the therapist to determine how much you can handle and at what pace you can proceed.

If you have panic attacks, your doctor may prescribe medications to boost your motivation to face your panic and all of that scary baggage that goes along with it. Drugs for panic disorder may help better with one of two different stages of panic: while you're anticipating anxiety or during the panic attack itself. Some medicines may help ease symptoms during both of these stages.

The most common medications prescribed for panic disorder are selective serotonin reuptake inhibitors (SSRIs) and benzodiazepines. Studies suggest that antidepressants can help 75 to 80 percent of people with panic disorder feel better. These medications include

> citalopram (Celexa)
> escitalopram (Lexapro)
> fluoxetine (Prozac)
> fluvoxamine (Luvox)
> paroxetine (Paxil)
> sertraline (Zoloft)

The ultimate success of treatment depends on you—are you willing to carefully follow your therapist's treatment plan? It may involve many steps, and it's not a magic instant cure, but if you hang in there, you should start to notice an improvement in your symptoms within three or four months of weekly sessions. If you keep up with your program, you should notice a major improvement after a year.

OBESITY AND EATING DISORDERS

Arlene was a friendly, outgoing teenager with lots of friends. But despite being on the basketball team, Arlene had been struggling with obesity for almost all of her life. What made it especially hard for her is that her father seemed to have a hard time accepting Arlene's size. The more weight she put on, the angrier her father seemed to get. An athlete and avid sportsman himself, her dad seemed almost embarrassed about Arlene's inability to keep her weight under control. In the face of her father's criticism, Arlene became more and more depressed about her situation. "I feel like he watches everything I put into my mouth," she said. "And nothing I ever do is good enough for him."

What made matters worse is that when Arlene went on a strict low-carbohydrate diet and lost 15 pounds, her father acted much more kindly toward her. This only proved to her that her dad loved her only when she was thin and fit—his ideal of a good daughter—and she slipped further into depression. The more she ate and the more she compulsively hoarded treats in her bedroom, the more unhappy she became.

Ultimately, she went to see the family doctor, who referred her for counseling to a local psychologist. It was clear to him, the doctor said, that Arlene's weight wasn't just about her diet or her genetic makeup; he could see that she was also clinically depressed and struggling with her relationship with her father, which only exacerbated her eating problem. She ate not because she was hungry but to fill up the empty feeling inside. Unless her depression was treated, he realized, her weight issues would never go away.

In our thinness-obsessed society, it's not surprising that obese teens are more likely to be ignored or treated in a degrading manner. What's more, studies have found that teens who report the highest number of these uncomfortable experiences are 11 times more likely to be depressed. However, it's not at all clear whether obesity leads to depression or whether depression leads to obesity. Many experts suspect it's just a repetitive cycle of depression and overeating: You're unhappy, so you eat to feel better, but then you gain more weight and you feel bad, so you eat to feel better, and so on. It's clear that for some teens, weight gain has as much to do with feelings and eating behavior as it does what you eat.

Obesity treatment. In treating eating disorders and depression at the same time, what typically works best is a combination of sensible diet and psychotherapy with a sensitive counselor, along with a brief course of antidepressants. The antidepressants help stabilize the brain chemicals, while counseling allows you to work through issues and feelings.

Eating disorders. You may know someone with an eating disorder, or perhaps you have such a problem yourself. If so, you're not alone: About 1 percent of teenage girls develop anorexia nervosa, a dangerous condition in which they can literally starve themselves to death. Another 2 or 3 percent develop bulimia nervosa, a destructive pattern of overeating followed by vomiting or purging.

In many cases, girls who develop eating disorders are first depressed. In fact, because so many girls with eating disorders also are depressed, some scientists believe there's a link between the two problems. They've found that brain chemicals serotonin and norepinephrine are abnormal in both those suffering from depression and those with eating disorders. It's not surprising that research also suggests that some patients with anorexia may respond well to the antidepressant medication fluoxetine (Prozac), which boosts the levels of the same chemicals in the brain that go awry in a person with eating disorders.

Treatment of eating disorders. An eating disorder can be a serious problem that is fatal in one out of every 10 cases, so the earlier treatment can begin, the better. The longer abnormal eating behaviors persist, the harder it is to overcome the disorder and its effects on the body. This can be a problem with anorexia, since girls with this problem often deny that there is any difficulty until they become so thin that it's impossible for family and friends to ignore.

The first step in treating an eating disorder is to determine how serious it is; a very serious case may require hospitalization, but most patients can be treated as outpatients. The combination of eating disorders and depression requires a comprehensive treatment plan involving a number of experts, including a physician, a dietary specialist, and a mental health expert.

Psychotherapy is typically recommended to treat the eating disorder and the underlying emotional issues and depression. Group therapy is particularly effective for teens with bulimia; in addition, individual or family therapy and cognitive-behavioral therapy is quite effective. Cognitive-behavioral therapists focus on changing eating behaviors usually by rewarding or modeling wanted behavior. These therapists also help patients work to change the distorted and rigid thinking patterns associated with eating disorders.

In addition, medications in combination with some type of psychotherapy are most effective in treating both the depression and the eating disorder. This combination of treatments also can help prevent a relapse once the medication is stopped.

POST-TRAUMATIC STRESS DISORDER (PTSD)

Like thousands of other people, Sharon survived the hurricane in New Orleans only to be haunted by post-traumatic stress disorder (PTSD). Losing her home and all of her friends at the local high school, she was moved with her mother out of state to live with relatives. In addition to the PTSD with which she still struggles, she developed depression as a result of her living situation.

This is not at all uncommon among kids with PTSD, who may develop depression and start to act out. Their schoolwork may suffer and their grades may begin to slide. PTSD is a condition that can develop after any life-threatening event, triggering frightening thoughts and memories, emotional numbness, and depression. Any teen who has been exposed to a traumatic event the way that Sharon has can develop PTSD, although many people do not.

If this happens to you, you may reexperience the event by having nightmares or by having constant thoughts about what happened. You might want to avoid places or events related to the trauma, and you'll probably feel numb. If you're a teen who has experienced a traumatic event, you may notice more headaches and tension, unexplained rashes, or problems with appetite and sleep. You may feel agitated or apathetic.

Treatment. Although most lucky teens improve on their own, some kids who aren't treated will still experience PTSD symptoms years after the event. That's why it's important to get treated as quickly as possible if you do develop PTSD. But there are some things you can do on your own to help restore a sense of control after a traumatic event. First, let yourself have the time to mourn or recover from the event, and don't be too hard on yourself during this period. Try to resume normal daily activities, eat a balanced diet, exercise, and surround yourself with family and friends. It's not unusual to feel shame, guilt, or even a numb feeling after a traumatic event. You might feel angry at yourself and wonder if you couldn't have done more to avoid the situation.

It may be tempting to try to deaden your emotional pain or stress, but try to avoid alcohol and drugs. It's not unusual for teens (and adults) to feel out of control after something traumatic occurs. Many feel angry, and they assume that drinking too much or taking drugs will make them feel better. It really only makes the problems you're coping with much worse.

Don't be afraid to ask for help from people who love you and who will listen and empathize. Or start a diary of your thoughts and feelings. Check out local support groups designed to help people who have experienced a trauma; you may find it easier to talk to people you don't know.

If in addition to your PTSD symptoms you also feel depressed, you'll probably need to talk to a mental health professional. You may feel overwhelming melancholy that interferes with your schoolwork, your family life, or your friends. Unfortunately, many people with PTSD often don't get help. Moreover, many traumatized people just don't feel like talking about their problems, because dealing with anything related to the event makes them feel even more uncomfortable. If this is happening to you, you really should talk with your parents about visiting an experienced mental health professional who can help you deal with your response to extreme stress.

Mental health professionals are trained to work with teens who have been affected by trauma, helping them find constructive ways of dealing with the depression. At the therapist's office, kids and teens with PTSD can be helped by a combination of medications and careful psychotherapy. Treatment often includes family therapy, so that your therapist can help your parents understand what PTSD symptoms mean. In fact, research shows that the better your parents can support you, the quicker you'll recover.

In some cases, a brief course of medication in addition to therapy can be helpful. Studies have found that several types of medication, particularly the selective serotonin reuptake inhibitors and other antidepressants, can be effective in treating a combination of depression and PTSD. As these medications ease serious symptoms of depression and anxiety, you'll be better able to cope with school and the pressures of everyday life while you work with your therapist. Medication is often used as a temporary measure until people with PTSD feel better.

SELF-ABUSE (CUTTING)

When Briana started coming to school in long sleeves, her friends didn't notice until one day the troubled teen showed her best friend bright-red slashes across her wrist. "I've been cutting myself," she confessed. Life at home was unbearable, she said. Her parents didn't understand her; they were always yelling at her and calling her names. She didn't like herself and was desperately unhappy and seriously depressed. Cutting herself somehow made her feel better, she told her friend. But she realized it wasn't normal, and she was embarrassed about the scars. Hence, the long sleeves.

Deliberately hurting yourself by scratching or cutting the skin is called cutting. It's a type of self-injury that's more common among girls, although some guys also injure themselves. People may cut themselves on the wrist, arm, leg, or stomach; others burn the skin with the end of a cigarette or lighted match. Kids who cut themselves usually try to hide the cuts and marks from their parents and teachers, and sometimes even from their closest friends.

Maybe you know someone who cuts—or maybe you've been feeling so depressed that you've started hurting yourself. Although it's not particularly common behavior, as more and more teens talk about cutting and people they know who do it, more and more teens may try it to feel better. Because it seems a little bit dangerous or forbidden, some younger teens may think that cutting will make them seem daring, grown up, or popular. A few crave attention—any kind of attention—and they like the notoriety that cutting brings them. As more kids talk about it and more books are written featuring girls who cut, the problem has almost begun to seem like a teenage fad, but it can be deadly serious.

While cutting may help you feel a bit better, at least at first, even most people who cut agree it's not the best way to get relief. Cutting doesn't make those sad feelings go away—it just temporarily pushes them aside. Most people who cut don't mean to damage themselves permanently, but it can happen. A person might not realize how deeply she's cut herself or might accidentally slice across the artery in the wrist. The cuts might be so deep that they require stitches or hospitalization. If the person uses something dirty to cut, the wounds can get infected.

Even worse, cutting can become a habit—the cutter begins to feel as if she has to do it to feel less depressed. This is because the brain links the cutting to the sense of relief from depression and craves this relief the next time depression gets unbearable. Once cutting becomes addictive like this, it's very hard to stop.

Kids cut themselves because they haven't developed healthy ways of dealing with depression, intense pressure, or upsetting relationships. Healthy ways of handling problems like these include talking to someone you trust, such as your parents, other adults, or friends. Often, kids who cut don't think they can talk to anyone about the way they feel. They may feel no one can help make their depression go away, and to them, cutting seems like the only way to ease these feelings. Cutting also can be a sign of mental health problems in addition to depression that may make the person impulsive or take unnecessary risks. Some kids who cut themselves have problems with drug or alcohol abuse.

Treatment. Kids can learn to stop cutting when they find better ways to deal with their depression or other problems. The first step—and the hardest one—is to confide in an adult about what you're doing. You might decide to talk to your mother or father, but if you don't feel comfortable doing that, talk to a school counselor, teacher, your coach, your doctor, or the school nurse. If you don't think you can face the person, write a note.

Explain that you've been cutting and you want to stop—and that you need help to do it. Keep asking for help until someone listens. Sometimes adults assume that cutting is just a phase that you'll outgrow. Sometimes adults (especially parents) don't like to think that their child might have a problem or might need therapy. If this happens, talk to a school counselor or nurse who can intervene on your behalf with your parents. Especially if your cutting is linked to depression, there are treatments that will help most kids who are depressed. Cutting is usually treated by a combination of medication and cognitive-behavioral therapy or interpersonal therapy. Once your depression is under control, your cutting may disappear—or you may need to spend more time with a therapist working on these issues. In any case, cutting is not a phase and not something you can handle on your own. Most people with depression need to work with a mental health professional to sort through feelings and to learn how to cope with stress. Cutting can be hard to stop, but it's certainly possible—and the sooner treatment is started, the easier cutting is to treat.

BULLYING

Tim was the class underdog who never quite seemed to be able to make friends the way the other kids did. His lack of social skills meant that he usually said or did the wrong thing, and his inability to fit in throughout elementary school made him a classic target for the school's bullies. Things only got much worse in middle school, where a couple of older bullies really made his life miserable. They taunted him for his unfashionable clothes and for his nerdy appearance and teased him unmercifully about his clumsiness on the basketball court. As things went from bad to worse, Tim became more and more depressed. He didn't tell anyone about his humiliating experiences at school, and he had no idea how to make it all stop. He began to believe the taunts his tormentors would yell at him—that he was stupid, worthless, and a geek. His depression deepened as his self-worth plummeted, but then his tormentors physically attacked him one day in the empty gym, and a teacher caught them. The bullies were expelled, and once the adults learned about Tim's experiences, they also realized how seriously depressed he had become and referred him for mental health treatment.

If you've ever been bullied like Tim, you know exactly how it feels. Bullies can tease, threaten, steal from you, or stalk you. They may bully in more subtle ways, by spreading malicious gossip or rumors and by intentionally excluding you. Sometimes their behavior may include violence, and the bully may physically or sexually attack the victim. As a result, the target may become socially rejected and isolated.

This happens on a weekly basis to about one of every 10 school-children across America. It tends to be worse in middle school, where up to 80 percent of students bully. Boys tend to bully others with physical threats or outright violence, whereas girls tend to bully by using cruel words and spreading gossip. Cyber-bullying by both boys and girls in online chat rooms, e-mail, and text-messaging is becoming more widespread, since it's far easier to get away with this type of behavior.

Bullies choose their targets in out-of-the-way spots where adults won't be likely to notice, such as on playgrounds, in lunchrooms and bathrooms, on school buses, or in unsupervised halls. This kind of harassment often leads to depression and low self-esteem, and the activities can be truly traumatizing. What makes it even worse is that once a kid is being bullied, he or she often loses social status, and former friends abandon him or her because they don't want to lose status by associating with the target—they don't want to risk getting bullied themselves.

Treatment. Seeking professional assistance early can lessen the risk of lasting emotional consequences. Luckily, there are some things you can do yourself if you're being harassed:

> ▶ Don't blame yourself for what has happened. Instead, look the bully in the eye and firmly and clearly tell him to stop. Then get away from the situation as quickly as possible.
> ▶ Tell a teacher or parent what happened right away. Don't just say, "I'm getting picked on at school." Tell exactly what's happening, how often it happens, who's involved, who sees it, and where it happens. You should also explain anything you've tried to do on your own.
> ▶ Don't give up. If a teacher says: "Oh, that's just normal boy behavior," find another adult to confide in. Don't accept the fact that any adult brushes off the bully's behavior. Keep on talking about the bullying until someone listens.
> ▶ Get help from your teacher, the school guidance counselor, or school administrators. They must follow school policy about bullying.
> ▶ If your school doesn't have a policy about bullying, ask your administrators (or have your parents ask) to check out programs that other schools and communities have used to help stop bullying, such as peer mediation, conflict resolution, anger management training, and better adult supervision. Have your

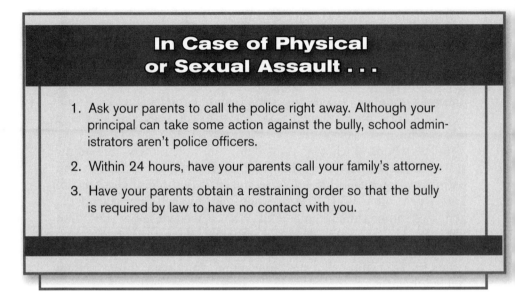

In Case of Physical or Sexual Assault . . .

1. Ask your parents to call the police right away. Although your principal can take some action against the bully, school administrators aren't police officers.

2. Within 24 hours, have your parents call your family's attorney.

3. Have your parents obtain a restraining order so that the bully is required by law to have no contact with you.

parents suggest that a mental health professional might help the school develop a strategy to deal with the bullying.

➤ Next, write letters to school board members separately and the superintendent after each incident. Give your school a reasonable amount of time to work out minor problems.

➤ Document what happened by taping statements of witnesses and having them sign statements about what they saw. Take photos of any injuries.

➤ If the bullying doesn't stop, ask your parents to write letters to your state representatives to explain what's happening in your school and how your administrators are handling your case.

Many kids who have been bullied still suffer once their bullies are dealt with—even if they've been expelled. Feelings of depression may linger. In these cases, it's a good idea to get your parents to arrange for you to see a therapist so you can deal with your depression and work through any remaining feelings.

WHAT YOU NEED TO KNOW

➤ Depression can be a by-product of other mental health problems, including anxiety and panic, obesity, cutting and self-abuse, and post-traumatic stress disorder.

➤ A combination of panic and anxiety disorders along with depression responds in most cases to a combination of medication and carefully targeted psychotherapy.

➤ Eating disorders and depression are treated with a combination of sensible diet and psychotherapy with a sensitive counselor, along with a brief course of antidepressants.

➤ Depression is common among kids with PTSD, who can be treated with sensitive psychotherapy and sometimes medication.

➤ Deliberately hurting yourself by scratching or cutting the skin is called cutting; it's more common among girls, although some guys also injure themselves. Cutting is usually treated by a combination of medication and cognitive-behavioral therapy or interpersonal therapy.

➤ If you're a victim of bullying, talk to your parents and school administrators; you may want to seek counseling as well.

9

Coping with Depression: Helping Out a Friend

Carla, 14, had been worried about her friend Chloe for some time. Chloe had had some eating problems in early middle school, and now her unhappiness just seemed to be getting worse day by day. Soon she was coming to school with stories of cutting herself, hiding the scars on her arms underneath long-sleeved sweaters. As Chloe's sadness worsened, Carla talked to her friend about her feelings. When Chloe insisted she didn't want to talk to her parents, Carla didn't give up. She encouraged her friend to go to their favorite teacher to talk about what she was experiencing. Eventually Chloe did, and the teacher referred Chloe to the principal, who called in Chloe's parents. Chloe received counseling from a therapist and, with intensive therapy and medication, is recovering slowly from her depression. Had it not been for her friend's intervention, it's not likely that Chloe would have spoken to any adult and would probably still be suffering needlessly.

Depression can rob a person of the happiness that comes along with doing everyday activities, hanging out with friends, going to the movies, or listening to music. Depression can fill a person with feelings of sadness and despair so devastating that it may seem as if there's no way to recover. It wouldn't be surprising if the depression of a close friend affected you, too, because you care about that person. But if you've never been depressed yourself, it's hard to understand how helpless and hopeless a person can feel.

Depressive disorders can make someone feel tired, worthless, helpless, and without hope. Some kids become so burdened by negative

111

thoughts and depressing feelings that they feel like giving up. Some kids turn to drugs or alcohol to try to make themselves feel better; others use razors or scissors to cut their skin. Depression can lead to eating disorders in still other kids. Some kids may think about or talk about committing suicide because they think life's not worth living or that no one cares about them. If you notice these negative behaviors and ideas in a friend, it's important to realize that they are part of the depression and usually don't accurately reflect the actual circumstances.

As the friend or relative of a depressed teenager, you'll probably want to help the person you care about. But you should realize that people rarely "snap out of" depression, so just begging them to feel better or pull themselves together isn't going to help. Nor should you accuse your friend of faking it or trying to get attention.

Remember that depression is an illness, just like cancer or diabetes. It's not a moral failure that someone can conquer if they only try hard enough. People who are depressed can't simply pull themselves together and feel better. It takes time and treatment. Would you ask your best friend, just diagnosed with cancer, to snap out of it? Of course not. Eventually, with the right treatment, most kids do get better. Keep that in mind, and keep reassuring the depressed person that with time and help, things will get better.

Get them help. The most important thing you can do for a depressed person is to help him or her get an appropriate diagnosis and treatment. If you suspect depression, gently urge your friend to see a doctor; it's the best thing you can do. Point out that depression is a medical problem that doctors can treat. You might say something like this: "How about if we go to the school counselor together and talk about how you've been feeling? We could just go and hear what she has to say."

With luck, your friend will agree. But what happens if your friend just doesn't want help or gets angry if you've suggested it? Perhaps your friend may not realize he or she is depressed. Maybe your friend is embarrassed about the way he or she is feeling or figures things will never get better. Most kids worry about betraying a friend's trust or ratting on a buddy, but the fact is that untreated depression can be dangerous. It's important that you tell an adult you trust about what's been going on. This person can then contact your friend's parents, and they can take things from there.

Offer emotional support. The second most important thing you can do is to offer emotional support by being understanding, patient, loving, and encouraging. Sometimes talking to a friend who's depressed may seem difficult—you may worry that you'll say the wrong thing or make your friend feel more uncomfortable. But even if you don't know what depression feels like, you can be empathetic and compassionate. Simply being there for the person can make a difference. Talk to your depressed friend and listen carefully. If she says, "I'll never have a boyfriend! Everyone I know has someone except for me. I'm just stupid and ugly!" try to remember that it's the depression talking. Respond patiently, but don't disparage her feelings: "I know it must seem that way, but most of the kids in our school aren't going out with anyone. And you're earning mostly As and Bs, so you can't be stupid!" Point out realities and offer hope.

Acknowledge your depressed friend's feelings, but try not to say, "I know how you feel." Most likely you can't really understand how deeply unhappy your friend is. Although you may think you know what's making your friend depressed, don't offer a solution or try to talk him or her out of these feelings. Just acknowledge the pain and sadness the person is feeling. Listen if your friend wants to talk, but try not to ask too many intrusive questions, because people who are depressed often don't have the energy or inclination to discuss their symptoms and may instead just stop talking.

Depressed people often feel worthless, or they may criticize themselves too much and ignore their own abilities. Remind your friend how much he or she means to you. Try not to be judgmental—what your friend really needs is for you to listen and to help him or her understand that he or she isn't alone.

If your friend is getting treatment, encourage him or her to continue it until symptoms begin to improve (this can take several weeks). You may need to encourage the person to seek different treatment if the depression doesn't improve.

Get help. It can be enormously stressful to try to help a depressed friend or family member, and you probably can't handle it all by yourself. Your friend or loved one may want you to keep the situation a secret, but secrets aren't healthy. Keeping quiet also means you'll be carrying a heavy burden, so try to gather together a small circle of other family members and friends to help.

Remember that your friend or family member needs professional help to get better; you shouldn't expect to be able to cure depression by yourself.

Do things together. Try to remember that just because someone is depressed, he or she is still your friend. Invite the person out for a walk, to the movies, or just to hang out at home and watch a movie or listen to music. Be gently insistent if the person refuses your invitation.

Encourage your friend to participate in activities that he or she once enjoyed, such as ice skating, basketball, swimming, or going to see a band. However, don't push the depressed person to undertake too much too soon. While depressed people do need someone to take their minds off their problems, too many demands can make them feel like more of a failure.

Handling substance abuse. A lot of depressed teenagers also have problems with alcohol or other drugs. You can encourage your friend to listen to the doctor's orders about not using drugs or alcohol. This may take some tact, since it's hard to do this without coming across in a condescending or preachy way. Usually the best way to handle this is to stick to the facts: "You know, Kurt, drinking or drugs can make you feel even more depressed" or "Cheryl, using alcohol or drugs to feel better can make you depend on that stuff to feel good—and then you've got two problems!" Or you could try "You know, I've heard that drinking or doing drugs can just make things worse. Why don't you talk to somebody about it?"

The depressed person's reaction to your initial comment will probably be a good indication of how receptive the person will be to what you're saying. Some kids might be ready to hear what you're saying, but others will just shut you off. If that happens, it's probably not going to do any good to pursue the issue. However, if the person does seem willing to listen, it may help if you express personal fears about what may happen. A comment such as "It's just that I really worry when you drink so much, because I know that you've been having a rough time lately" shows concern without sounding superior or preachy.

Ask what you can do. Your friend may not really know, but at least if you ask, he or she will know that you're trying to help. Depression may mean your friend is having trouble taking care of chores or duties. See if you can lend a hand to help your friend out.

Offer encouragement. Often someone who's depressed just doesn't feel like getting out of bed or leaving the house; as a result, most kids who are depressed isolate themselves. That can only make things worse, however. If this is happening to your friend, try gently encouraging the person to get up and get dressed. Offer to take a walk together, or invite your friend out to a movie—anything to get the person out of the house. However, you'll want to be encouraging, not forceful. You may think your friend needs to go to counseling or be more active, and you may be right, but putting pressure on a depressed person can backfire. The depressed person may dig in his or her heels and refuse your help or may only go through the motions of doing whatever you're suggesting. On the inside, he or she may still have the same attitudes, beliefs, and behavior patterns. If the person really digs in and doesn't want to leave the house, don't make demands. Remember that someone who's depressed already feels overwhelmed, so if you're constantly nagging or pushing, the person might retreat even more and push you away. If your friend turns down your invitations, accept it. Wait a bit, and then gently ask again.

IF YOUR MOM OR DAD IS DEPRESSED

Anyone can be depressed, anytime, at any age. Depression might affect your mother or father, and if it is, it's going to have a big impact on your life, too. Watching a parent struggle with depression can be frustrating and downright frightening—after all, this is the person who's supposed to take care of you. When you're depressed, it can be hard to get up and go about everyday life. Your mother might not be able to make you breakfast before school, or your father might stop throwing a football around with you on the weekends. Maybe you notice your parents drinking more than they used to.

It can be hard to talk to your parent about these kinds of symptoms, but it's important to discuss how you're feeling and what you suspect. If your parents won't discuss your worries, don't give up. Instead, see if you can confide in another adult you trust—maybe a grandparent or an aunt or uncle, someone at your school, or a close friend of your parents. If their behavior is bothering you and it's affecting your life, you need to talk to someone and try to get help. Of course, you can't take responsibility for your mother's or father's life—the decision to get help is up to them. But there are things you can do to help.

If you decide to talk to your parent about depressed behavior, start by being positive. Instead of using "you" sentences ("You seem depressed a lot" or "You aren't getting out of bed these days"), try the "I" approach: "I love you, but I'm worried about what's been going on around here" or "I love you and I want you to feel better." Point out that new treatments can help most people feel better, but not getting treatment means that the situation at home won't improve and may get worse.

Because depression often affects the ability to deal with everyday life, you may need to help out more around the house for a while, taking on more of the household chores, taking care of your little brother or sister, or doing the food shopping. It's best if you can do things with your mother or father, rather than always doing things for them.

It can be very hard if a member of your family is depressed—especially your parent. Living with someone who's depressed can be incredibly difficult, and you may start feeling stressed and depressed, too. If your parent gets angry with you or acts uncharacteristically, try not to take those actions personally—they aren't directed at you, even if it feels like they are. You may feel guilty, frustrated, angry, or tired of coping with your parent's depression—and that's certainly understandable. But remember that you didn't cause your parent's depression and you're not responsible for fixing the problem—so don't try to "rescue" him or her. Try to let go of those uncomfortable emotions. It may help if you talk about your feelings with a support group or discuss the situation with a counselor, a relative, another friend, or a trusted teacher.

Remember that looking out for a depressed parent can be over-whelming—after all, you're still a kid! It's important that you plan some time for yourself so you can do things that you enjoy. Get out of the house, go for a walk, or catch a movie or dinner with your friends.

Of course, being depressed is extremely difficult, and you may feel guilty or selfish for thinking about yourself or trying to have some fun. But taking care of yourself is vital, because if you don't, you'll burn out—and that won't help either of you. Remember that while there's a lot you can do to help your depressed parent, you can't do everything, and you can't cure depression yourself. You can't watch the person 24 hours a day or become responsible for how the person lives his or her life. Your mother or father must take the responsibility to get better.

IF SOMEONE THREATENS SUICIDE

If one of your friends is already depressed or showing some signs of depression, one bad problem (such as parents getting a divorce or a breakup with a girlfriend or boyfriend) can trigger suicidal behavior. People consider suicide when they are hopeless and can't see alternative solutions to their problems. Suicidal behavior is most often related to depression or to alcohol or other substance abuse, but it's also more likely to occur after stressful events. However, people whose suicide seems to have been triggered by a particular event often have significant underlying depression that may not have been noticed, even by family and friends.

Although teen suicide is never a solution to any problem or unhappy feeling, it's the third leading cause of death for kids aged 15 to 24, surpassed only by car accidents and homicide. Suicide attempts are even more common. Suicide rates spike during adolescence for many reasons, including access to lethal weapons and drugs and alcohol.

If you have a friend who talks about suicide or shows some suicide warning signs don't ignore the situation. Even if you think your friend is just showing off or trying to get attention, talk about those suicidal thoughts with him or her. Although not everyone who talks about suicide actually makes an attempt, it's not true that people who talk about suicide won't really try it. That's why it's important to take every suicide threat seriously.

Many people think they should ignore such comments or simply dismiss the comments by saying, "You don't mean that!" and then changing the subject. Talking about suicide will not somehow give the person ideas that weren't there in the first place. In fact, for some teens at risk of depression, talking about suicide may even make them feel better—at least a little bit. Most of the time, people considering suicide will talk about it if someone they care about asks them.

Risk factors. If you're wondering whether a friend or family member is at risk for suicide, the risk goes up if the teen

- is struggling with problems beyond his or her control, such as divorce, alcoholism in the family, or domestic violence
- has experienced physical or sexual abuse
- doesn't get along with his or her parents
- feels helpless or worthless
- uses alcohol or drugs to try to numb the emotional pain
- doesn't have much support or many friends
- is socially isolated or rejected by people at school or in the community
- has a family history of depression or suicide
- has homosexual feelings and doesn't have any support at home, at school, or in the community
- expresses feelings violently
- has been teased or tormented, especially if the teasing has a homophobic theme

How to talk about it. Asking a friend about suicide can be very hard to do, especially if he or she hasn't brought up the topic—but it's very important. You may have to get over some discomfort of your own in order to discuss your friend's feelings. Sometimes it helps to let your friend know why you're asking. For instance, you might say; "I've noticed that you seem really sad all the time. You don't seem to want to do anything with us anymore. Are you having a tough time? Are things so bad that you might think about hurting yourself?"

If your friend comes right out and talks about death, you could say; "I've noticed that you talk a lot about wanting to die. Have you been really thinking about trying to kill yourself?" Or, you can be even more direct: "Are you thinking about killing yourself?"

By gently encouraging your friend to talk about suicidal thoughts, you can help your friend feel less alone, less isolated, and more cared about and understood. Many depressed people become suicidal because they see no way out of their problems or their black outlook, they don't think anyone cares about them, or they feel that they'd be better off dead. Helping your friend realize that people do care and that suicide may not be the answer could save a life. Talking also may give the person a chance to discover another solution to the situation.

If you feel that you just can't ask these questions, then find someone who can, but don't ignore a friend who you think is contemplating suicide.

How to respond. If your friend does confess to having suicidal thoughts, try not to respond angrily, abruptly, or with a negative opinion. Don't say, "Well, that's just stupid!" or "Only losers kill themselves." Listen without judging, and reassure the person that you still care. Most likely, your friend needs someone to listen. Don't joke about the person's worries, and don't assume that you know what the person is going through. Just listen. If you think your friend may attempt suicide very soon, try to make sure he or she isn't left alone.

Tell an adult. If a friend threatens suicide, you'll need to report the conversation to an adult as soon as possible. Sure, you may have visions of trying to help your friend by yourself, but it's always safest to get help. If you know the depressed person's therapist, you can contact that person directly. (This route might be easier if the depressed person is a family member.)

If the depressed person is your friend, you may feel uncomfortable calling your friend's therapist, whom you probably don't know. Instead, you could confide in a trusted teacher, a school counselor or psychologist, or the school principal. Some schools maintain an anonymous reporting system that allows you to submit a note detailing your concerns about a fellow student. In almost all school suicide and school homicide situations, the kids who committed the acts had previously told friends about their intentions, but their friends didn't tell any adults. Lives might have been saved if friends had only intervened.

Even if your friend swore you to secrecy and you feel like telling is a betrayal, you should still seek help. Yes, you'll be breaking a confidence, but sometimes you have to take that risk to help a friend. Even doctors must break confidences if it means saving a life. Share your concerns with an adult you trust as soon as possible.

Take action! If your friend is threatening to kill himself, don't leave the person alone. Remove any weapons or large amounts of medication and call a suicide hotline or your friend's therapist. In a crisis, call emergency services. You can call a local emergency number (911) or the toll-free National Suicide Prevention Lifeline at 1-800-273-8255 (TTY: 1-800-799-4889). This number can be used anywhere in the United States—by either a person contemplating suicide or someone like you worried about a suicidal friend—and it automatically connects you to a certified crisis center near where your call was placed. The National Suicide Prevention Lifeline's mission is to provide immediate help to someone in suicidal crisis by connecting the person to the nearest available suicide prevention and mental health service provider. It's the only national suicide prevention and intervention telephone resource funded by the federal government.

Alternatively, you can check out the Web site for the U.S. National Suicide Hotlines at http://suicidehotlines.com/national.html, which offers a list of hotlines around the country. If you don't have access to the Internet, you can look for a local suicide crisis number in your phone book.

If a family member, such as your mother or father, is suicidal, you must get help. Most states allow a doctor or psychologist to hospitalize people against their will if they are in danger of hurting themselves or someone else. The emergency hospitalization doesn't usually last very long, just long enough for the doctors to assess your parent's depression. After 24 to 72 hours, the patient and a representative from the hospital attend a hearing in court, and the judge determines if the patient has to stay in the hospital for a longer period.

You may be reluctant to force a parent into the hospital, but if your mother or father is at risk of suicide, you need to intervene. Even if your parent gets upset with you, you may have to do so.

WHAT YOU NEED TO KNOW

> - Depressive disorders can make someone feel tired, worthless, helpless, and without hope; they can trigger substance abuse, cutting, or eating disorders.
> - The most important thing to do for a depressed person is to tell a trusted adult what's been going on; the person can then contact your friend's parents, and they can take things from there.
> - It's also important to be understanding, patient, loving, and encouraging.
> - Don't worry about saying the wrong thing or making your friend feel more uncomfortable; simply being there for the person can make a difference.
> - Invite the person out for a walk, to the movies, or just to hang out at home and watch a movie or listen to music.
> - Encourage your depressed friend not to use drugs or alcohol.
> - Ask what you can do to help and offer encouragement.
> - If your parent is depressed, it's important to discuss how you're feeling and what you suspect.
> - If your parent won't discuss his or her depression, confide in another adult you trust.
> - When talking to your parents about their depression, use sentences starting with "I" ("I think there might be a problem") rather than the more accusatory "you" ("You seem depressed").
> - Living with someone who's depressed can be incredibly difficult, and you may start feeling stressed and depressed, too.
> - If your depressed parent gets angry with you, try not to take it personally.
> - You didn't cause your parent's depression and you're not responsible for fixing the problem, so don't try to "rescue" him or her.
> - If your parent is depressed, taking care of yourself is vital, because if you don't, you'll burn out.
> - If one of your friends is already depressed or showing signs of depression, one extra bad problem can trigger suicidal behavior.

> ▶ Never ignore a friend who talks about suicide or shows suicide warning signs.
> ▶ If you suspect a friend is thinking about suicide, ask the person directly if this is the case, and listen compassionately; don't joke or criticize the person for feeling this way.
> ▶ If your friend threatens to commit suicide, don't leave the person alone; remove any weapons or medication and call a suicide hotline, your friend's therapist, or emergency services.

10

Paying for Care

You probably feel as if you've got enough problems in coping with your depression without having to worry about who's going to pay for your care—and it's true that health finances is an adult problem. Still, lots of older teens are aware of their family's financial problems. Many families have trouble paying for mental health care and antidepressant drugs because health insurance may not cover these items very well—if at all. Or maybe a friend of yours has confided that his medication is very expensive and he doesn't know how he's going to afford it.

Unfortunately, many families today are finding that getting good health care and paying for medications can be difficult. Because depression is usually treated with both therapy and medication, patients usually must visit both a psychologist and a psychiatrist for treatment—and the medications themselves aren't cheap. It's a major problem in the United States these days.

What do you do if your parents make too much money to qualify for Medicaid coverage but not enough to pay for your doctor visits, therapy, and medications? Fortunately, there are ways to get the care you, a family member, or a friend might need.

PSYCHOTHERAPY COSTS

Many health insurance companies don't offer benefits for psychotherapy. Some policies do cover a few visits a year, but they don't reimburse very much. Often, families are left trying to make up the difference between what their insurance company will pay and what the doctor charges. Families who don't have insurance at all face the full burden of mental health care costs. Since fees typically begin at about $75 for one 45-minute session, that can get expensive.

Medicaid. Medicaid is a state-run public health program that covers health care and transportation for people living in poverty who meet the maximum income limits. States are required to cover a core set of benefits, including hospital, outpatient, doctor services, and home health services. More information about eligibility requirements is available at local welfare and medical assistance offices. Your parents will need to check with your state Medicaid office to see precisely what is covered where you live and what the income limits are. You also can find information about Medicaid at http://www. CMS.gov, or call the Social Security Administration at 800-772-1213.

Low-cost health care clinics. Many communities have community mental health centers (CMHCs) that offer a range of mental health treatment and counseling services, usually at a lower rate for low-income people. CMHCs generally require that your family either have a private insurance plan or be receiving public assistance. If you need to find low- or no-cost health care, you or your parents can check with the federal bureau of the Health Resources and Services Administration (HRSA), which maintains a nationwide directory of clinics. For information, you can check out this Web site: http:// www.ask.hrsa.gov/pc. By typing in your state, city, and zip code and the type of clinic in which you're interested (in this case, "mental health/substance abuse services"), you can access a list of clinics in your neighborhood. Or you can contact the Community Mental Health Centers, National Council for Community Behavioral Health Care, at 301-984-6200 or visit their Web site at: http://www.nccbh. org. Alternatively, visit this Web site: http://www.mentalhealth. samhsa.gov/databases.

Finally, many states have a range of other programs that can help pay for mental health care issues for kids under age 19. Do a Web search for your state's programs and check out what's available for the Medicaid and Children's Health Insurance Program (CHIP).

Pastoral counseling. Your church or synagogue can connect your family with a pastoral counseling program. Certified pastoral counselors are ministers or rabbis who have advanced degrees in pastoral counseling, as well as professional counseling experience. Pastoral counseling is usually less expensive than traditional therapy and is often provided on a sliding scale depending on family income.

MEDICATION COSTS

If you've been diagnosed with depression, your doctor is probably going to prescribe an antidepressant for you. Many of the newest medications don't yet have generic versions available. At more than $3 per pill, antidepressants can be very pricey.

Even if your parents don't have insurance, or if their plan doesn't include a prescription drug benefit, don't assume that you won't be able to be treated. Your first option is simply to ask your doctor for free medication samples. (Often you don't even have to ask; if your doctor starts you out on one type of antidepressant to see how you do, he or she may simply give you some free samples to start you off.) If your doctor doesn't offer, have your parents ask whether any samples are available.

Of course, this doesn't usually work for the long term. Many kids take an antidepressant for at least a year, and you won't be able to get all your medications through free samples at the doctor's office. Luckily, you have another option.

Patient assistance programs. Most drug companies offer free medications to patients who can't afford them through a variety of patient assistance programs. Your parents may have to fill out some paperwork and jump through a few hoops to qualify, but once you do, you'll be assured a steady supply. Your doctor will usually need to send a note for you, and your parents will need to add proof of financial need, a statement that you don't have any health insurance, or a statement that you don't have a prescription drug benefit. Appendix 2 provides a list of some of these programs, organized by drug name.

Many doctors don't know about these special programs, so you'll need to do some investigating on your own. The easiest way to find these special programs is by surfing the Internet. Each drug company usually lists its own program online, so if you know the name of the company that makes your antidepressant, just search for the company's name and check out its Web site.

Some helpful Web sites dedicated to finding alternative medication sources make things easier for patients. Visit any of the Web sites listed below that provide information about patient assistance programs providing free prescription medications to eligible participants.

Free Medicine Foundation
http://www.freemedicinefoundation.com
The Free Medicine Foundation was set up by a corps of volunteers to help needy American families handle their prescription drug bills. The foundation is designed to help patients without prescription coverage, who have a low income, or who have used up all their prescription benefits. You can qualify if your family makes up to $38,000; in some cases, based on the size of your family, people with annual incomes up to $60,000 can still qualify.

The Medicine Program
http://www.themedicineprogram.com
This program offers a unique free discount prescription drug program, which is made possible by a special discount from companies that is available only to large groups and corporations. In this plan, everyone is eligible. This prescription plan is free of charge and is available to anyone trying to lower the cost of their prescription bills. Visit the Web site to print a free prescription card, present it at more than 35,000 participating pharmacies, and save up to 60 percent on medication.

Medicine Research Centers
(662) 513-5231
This organization ships free prescription medicine for you to your doctor's office. To qualify, you must not have Medicaid, any other state aid program, or prescription insurance coverage, and your parents' income must show that it would be a hardship for your family to pay full price for your medications.

NeedyMeds program
http://www.needymeds.com
NeedyMeds was established in 1997 as a source of free information on programs to help people obtain health supplies and equipment. This Web site offers new information, links, and information about the NeedyMeds Manual, a printed version of the information on the Web site.

Partnership for Prescription Assistance
(888) 477-2669
https://www.pparx.org/Intro.php
The Partnership for Prescription Assistance has gathered together drug companies, doctors and other health care providers, patient

organizations, and community groups to help qualifying patients get the medicines they need through public or private programs. The organizations collaborating on this program are the American Academy of Family Physicians, the American Autoimmune Related Diseases Association, Lupus Foundation of America, NAACP, National Alliance for Hispanic Health, and the National Medical Association.

Prescription Drug Assistance Programs
(800) 762-4636

http://www.phrma.org

At this Web site, you will find a directory where you can type in the name of the medication you need and receive the name of the corresponding patient assistance program for that medication. If your family qualifies, you can receive medication at no cost.

RxOutreach
http://www.rxassist.org

At RxAssist, you'll find a database of patient assistance programs run by drug companies that provide free medications to people who can't afford to buy their medicine. The site also offers practical tools, news, and articles so that health care professionals and patients can find the information they need.

Mail-order medications from Canada. Many Americans who are unable to afford medications at their corner pharmacy have started ordering less expensive versions from Canada through mail order. Although technically against U.S. law—and the government warns that there's no way to make sure these drugs are safe—consumer advocates insist it's a sensible choice.

If you and your parents choose to order your medications online, be sure to choose a reputable Web site. One way to make sure you get the best medications is by visiting Web sites run by states that have designed programs for their residents.

I-SaveRx
http://www.i-saverx.net

If you live in Illinois, Kansas, Missouri, Vermont, or Wisconsin, you can participate in I-SaveRx, a mail-order pharmacy program developed by the governors of these five states that provides mail-order access to cheaper brand-name prescription drugs from Canada, the United Kingdom, and Ireland. You must live in one of these states to participate.

Minnesota RXConnect

http://www.state.mn.us/portal/mn/jsp/home.do?agency = Rx

The Minnesota governor has set up a Web site to help residents find less expensive drugs from Canada and the United Kingdom.

New Hampshire

http://www.egov.nh.gov/medicine%2Dcabinet

It's not surprising that a state with the motto "Live free or die" would feel strongly about allowing its residents to order less expensive drugs from Canada. This Web Site offers a number of helpful sites and also offers a link to CanadaDrugs.com.

North Dakota

http://www.governor.state.nd.us/prescription-drug.html

North Dakota's Web page about Canadian drugs offers detailed explanations and links to Web sites to help you import medications.

WHAT YOU NEED TO KNOW

➤ Community mental health agencies, some private mental health professionals, and some family service agencies charge fees based on a patient's ability to pay.

➤ Community-based services offer a range of mental health treatment and counseling services at a reduced rate for low-income families.

➤ Affordable care may be provided by county mental health departments, school-based services, or a religious leader (pastoral counselor).

➤ Medicaid is a state-run public health program that may cover mental health care and transportation for people who live in poverty.

➤ Employee assistance programs for workers and their families cover brief treatments for mental health problems.

➤ Doctors may give you free samples of medications, and most drug companies also offer free medications to patients who can't afford them.

11

In the Future

In the past 20 years, science has made incredible strides in treating depression. When your parents were your age, there were not many effective treatments, and most kids simply didn't get the help they desperately needed. Today, experts estimate that one in eight teenagers still meets the definition of depressed, but unfortunately, far too many of them—about 70 percent—still don't ever get any kind of treatment, even though there are so many effective ones. Instead, these teens simply struggle through their adolescence amidst emotional turmoil, doing their best to make it through high school and on into adulthood. In the future, experts hope that society will do a much better job in identifying which teens are depressed and come up with even better ways to treat depression. Better diagnosis, treatment, and prevention are critical public health priorities.

Since the 1990s, scientists have made significant strides in the ability to investigate how brains function, and they hope to learn a lot more about how the brain regulates mood. As scientists slowly discover how genes are linked to proteins and how proteins affect nerve circuits and mental function, a clearer picture of depression will emerge. Once that happens, it will be much simpler to come up with specific treatments to repair specific problems in the brain.

Depression most likely is the result of a number of complex and interacting factors. Depressed people have different symptoms, experience depression differently, and react to treatments differently, which can make it hard to understand and treat the disorder. However, research may soon make it possible to identify effective treatments for individuals based on the kinds of symptoms they have. This would mean that one depressed person who can't sleep would get a different type of medication or treatment than a depressed person who can't get out of bed would.

GENETICS RESEARCH

Today experts believe that depression is a disorder of the brain that occurs when brain circuits responsible for regulating mood, thinking, sleep, appetite, and behavior go awry and when vital chemicals used by nerve cells to communicate fluctuate out of balance. Scientists also know that some cases of depression occur as a result of the influence of several genes interacting with environmental factors.

Researchers are quite sure that genes play an important role in the likelihood that a particular person will develop depression, and they are equally sure that it takes more than one gene. Instead, researchers believe that depression may be linked to many gene variants that act together in some way, with either a child's environment or his or her unique development. Many experts believe that genes affect the risk of depression by shaping a person's responses to stress. For example, people are more likely to become depressed in response to stress if they have a particular variant of a gene that influences serotonin; other studies have linked the same gene to alcohol abuse, anxiety disorders, and resistance to antidepressants.

Unfortunately, figuring out which genes are responsible has been extremely difficult. Once experts know more about the interaction between genes and depression, they'll be able to develop better drugs to treat depression.

The most immediate priority is to target today's drugs more effectively. For example, small variations in a person's genetic DNA sequence can have major effects in the body. For example, people with a variation called G1463A have very low levels of serotonin, the chemical involved in depression. This variation appears more often in people with major depressive disorder—and what's more, depressed people with the G1463A variation don't respond very well to antidepressants such as Prozac and Zoloft, which act on serotonin. Someday, your doctor could test you for G1463A to help figure out which antidepressant to prescribe.

ENVIRONMENT

The environment—the kind of place where you grew up and where you live and go to school—also has a significant impact on your personality and mental health. Even if you have a genetic tendency toward depression, if you grow up in a supportive, accepting environment, you may never develop a full-blown depression. On the other hand, if you don't have a predisposition to depression but you grow up in a hypercritical, demanding home, you may develop depressive symptoms anyway. In the future, the better we can teach people how to parent, the more likely we are to eliminate domestic violence and physical and sexual abuse, and the more likely the prevention of depression will be.

NEW THINKING ON DEPRESSION SUBTYPES

Researchers continue to look for distinct subtypes of depression that can be identified by genetic risk, symptoms, and course of illness. Scientists are also trying to identify simple biological markers of depression that can be detected in blood or in the brain. This type of biological marker could reveal a specific depression profile for each patient, which would help mental health experts select the most effective treatments.

ANTIDEPRESSANT RESEARCH

Although antidepressants have been used clinically for more than 50 years, no one knows exactly how they work. It is known that newer antidepressants work very well in the short term for depression, but there haven't been many longer studies that show whether the improvements in depression last and whether there are any adverse effects over the long term. This is especially important for young people.

As scientists learn how and where in the brain antidepressants work, they will be able to develop more potent medications that may help improve symptoms much more quickly than antidepressants do now. This would mean that patients wouldn't have to wait three or four weeks before their symptoms improve. And the more scientists understand about how these drugs work, the better they will know why different drugs produce side effects, so they'll be able to design new treatments with fewer side effects.

In particular, scientists are looking at the distinct biological problems that occur with different forms of depression and how different antidepressants work on these depression subtypes. Combinations of different drugs often work best in treating depression, by either enhancing the therapeutic action or reducing side effects. Although doctors often use these combination strategies, there's not much research that doctors can rely on when prescribing appropriate combination treatment.

Untreated depression often gets worse very quickly or leads to recurrent episodes that return more often and more severely over time. Scientists are studying whether early intervention with antidepressants and psychotherapy when a person is feeling well might prevent recurrence of depression.

ELECTROCONVULSIVE THERAPY (ECT)

Electroconvulsive therapy (ECT) is one of the most effective treatments for depression, but it's the one that carries the most stigma. Between 80 and 90 percent of people with severe depression improve dramatically with ECT, which produces a brain seizure in an anesthetized patient as a result of electrical stimulation to the brain. Repeated treatments are necessary to get the best response, but temporary memory loss and other thinking problems are common. Although some people report lasting problems, modern ECT techniques have reduced the side effects by lowering the electricity dose and altering the placement of electrodes. Although ECT is very effective for treating depression, however, many patients get worse again as soon as the treatments are stopped. New research is assessing the possibility of maintenance ECT treatments as a follow-up measure.

TEENAGE DEPRESSION

It appears from research studies that depression is occurring earlier in people born in more recent decades. Because depression that develops early in life often persists, recurs, and continues into adulthood, early-onset depression may mean that as an adult, the person will have more severe depression. As a result, diagnosing and treating teens who are depressed is very important as a way of preventing problems at school, with friends, and with behavior.

Unfortunately, research on the diagnosis and treatment of depression in teenagers hasn't kept pace with similar research in adults. Diagnosing depression in teens may be more challenging, since early symptoms can be dismissed as normal teenage moodiness. Treating depression in teens is also tricky because no research has established how safe and effective antidepressants are in this age group, and cases of suicide attempts related to antidepressant use in this group have been disturbing.

In fact, over the past few decades, the suicide rate in young people has increased dramatically. Currently, scientists are studying effective ways to prevent suicide in teenagers; at present, experts believe that early diagnosis and treatment of depression is probably the best way to prevent suicide.

Until recently, there wasn't much information about the safety and effectiveness of antidepressants in teens; instead, antidepressant doses for kids were based on adult standards. In fact, one recent government-funded study revealed that fluoxetine (Prozac) was safe and effective for kids and teens but that they didn't respond as well as did adults. This suggests that more research is needed into existing treatments and into developing even more effective medications and psychotherapies designed specifically for children.

HARD-TO-TREAT DEPRESSION
While up to 80 percent of people with depression respond very well to treatment, the rest just don't seem to get better on any drug or therapy. Among those who do respond to treatment, some will relapse. Others who do respond to antidepressants nevertheless suffer unpleasant side effects from these medications. This is why scientists continue to search for more effective treatments for depression that carry fewer side effects than the current medications.

HERBAL TREATMENTS
Although St. John's wort appears to work for mild depression, there haven't been many studies in this country to compare this herb both with placebos and with several other antidepressants in patients with severe depression. Studies also need to be done for the herbal depression remedies valeriana and kava kava. If ineffective, these nonprescription products could hurt depressed people by delaying effective treatment.

WHAT YOU NEED TO KNOW
> Research may soon make it possible for doctors to identify effective treatments for individuals based on the kinds of symptoms they have.
> Depression occurs when brain circuits responsible for regulating mood, thinking, sleep, appetite, and behavior go awry and when vital chemicals used by nerve cells to communicate are out of balance.
> Some cases of depression occur as a result of the influence of several genes interacting with environmental factors.
> Distinct subtypes of depression may one day be identified by genetic risk, symptoms, and course of illness.

➤ Scientists are also trying to identify simple biological markers of depression that can be detected in blood or in the brain, revealing a specific depression profile for each patient.

➤ Someday scientists may develop more potent medications that would improve symptoms much more quickly than antidepressants do now.

➤ Most people with severe depression improve dramatically with electroconvulsive treatment but get worse when treatments end; new research is investigating maintenance ECT treatments.

➤ Depression is occurring earlier in people born in more recent decades, and more research is needed to understand existing treatments and develop more effective medications and psychotherapies designed specifically for children and adolescents.

➤ More research is also needed to determine if herbal treatments for depression, such as St. John's wort, valeriana, and kava kava, are effective.

APPENDIX 1

Associations and Resources Related to Depression

ALCOHOL ABUSE
Chemically Dependent Anonymous
General Service Office
P.O. Box 423
Severna Park, MD 21146
(888) CDA-HOPE
http://www.cdaweb.org
CDA is a 12-step fellowship of men and women whose primary purpose is to stay clean and sober and to help others achieve recovery from chemical dependence. CDA deals entirely with the disease of addiction, without making distinctions in the recovery process based on any particular substance, believing that the addictive-compulsive usage of chemicals is the core of the disease and that the use of any mood-changing chemical will result in relapse.

National Clearinghouse for Alcohol and Drug Information
P.O. Box 2345
Rockville, MD 20847-2345
(800) 729-6686
(877) 767-8432 (Español)
(301) 468-2600
(800) 487-4899 (TTY)
http://www.health.org
The world's largest resource for current information and materials concerning alcohol and substance abuse prevention, intervention, and treatment. NCADI is a service of the Center for Substance Abuse Prevention and offers a wide variety of free services, including NCADI Information Services Department, the NCADI Library, and Prevention Pipeline.

SMART Recovery
7537 Mentor Avenue, Suite 306
Mentor, OH 44060
(866) 951-5357
(440) 951-5357
http://www.smartrecovery.org
SMART Recovery offers free face-to-face and online mutual help
groups. SMART Recovery (Self-Management And Recovery
Training) helps people recover from all types of addictive
behaviors, including alcoholism, drug abuse, substance abuse,
drug addiction, alcohol abuse, gambling addiction, cocaine
addiction, and addiction to other substances and activities.
SMART Recovery is an alternative to Alcoholics Anonymous and
Narcotics Anonymous and sponsors more than 300 face-to-face
meetings around the world and more than 16 online meetings
per week. In addition, its online message board is an excellent
forum in which to learn about SMART Recovery and seek support.
SMART Recovery is recognized by the American Academy of
Family Physicians, the Center for Health Care Evaluation, the
National Institute on Drug Abuse (NIDA), and the American
Society of Addiction Medicine.

Students Against Destructive Decisions
255 Main Street
Marlborough, MA 01752
(877) SADD-INC
http://www.sadd.org/contact.htm
Originally, the mission of SADD was to help young people say
no to drinking and driving. Today, the mission has expanded
because students say positive peer pressure, role models, and
other strategies can help them say no to more than drinking
and driving. As a result, SADD has become a peer leadership
organization dedicated to preventing destructive decisions,
particularly underage drinking, other drug use, impaired driving,
teen violence, and teen depression and suicide. SADD tries to
provide students with the best prevention and intervention tools
possible to deal with these destructive decisions.

ANXIETY
Anxiety Disorders Association of America
8730 Georgia Avenue, Suite 600
Silver Spring, MD 20910

(240) 485-1001
http://www.adaa.org
The ADAA promotes the prevention and cure of anxiety disorders
and works to improve the lives of all people who suffer from them.

The Anxiety & Panic Internet Resource
http://www.algy.com/anxiety/index.shtml
A self-help resource for those with anxiety disorders; provides
information and support for patients.

Anxiety Treatment Network of Southwest Michigan
http://www.anxietytreatmentnetwork.org
A free resource for those with anxiety disorders in southwest
Michigan, this Web site includes an online newsletter, information
about support groups, therapists, and presentations in the area, as
well as book reviews and links to national organizations such as
ADAA and Freedom From Fear. The network encourages the use
of research-based approaches for the treatment and prevention of
anxiety disorders.

Childhood Anxiety Network
3741 Locke Lane
Prospect, KY 40059
http://www.childhoodanxietynetwork.org
The Childhood Anxiety Network was developed to supply information
about various childhood anxieties. The group's primary mission
is to educate as well as to advocate the early diagnosis of anxiety
disorders.

Freedom From Fear
308 Seaview Avenue
Staten Island, NY 10305
(718) 351-1717 (ext. 24)
http://www.freedomfromfear.org
A national nonprofit mental health advocacy association. The
mission of FFF is to improve the lives of all those affected by
anxiety, depressive, and related disorders through advocacy,
education, research, and community support. The online FFF
has developed an anxiety and depression screening program
with a free consultation from a health care professional. The
organization offers research, outreach education, public TV
ventures, training programs for health care workers, and
government lobbying.

Psychological Self-Help
http://mentalhelp.net/psyhelp
Psychological Self-Help is a Web site that covers all kinds of problems in the anxiety area, including trauma, stress, anxiety, fears, worry, shyness, obsession-compulsions, and various health and pain disorders.

BIPOLAR DISORDER
Canadian Network for Mood and Anxiety Treatments
http://www.canmat.org/canmat
Canadian Network for Mood and Anxiety Treatments is an academically based not-for-profit research organization linking health care professionals from across Canada who have a special interest in mood and anxiety disorders. The ultimate goal of CANMAT is to improve the quality of life of persons suffering from mood and anxiety disorders through innovative research projects and registries, development of evidence-based and best-practice educational programs, and guideline and policy development. Formed in 1995, CANMAT is an independent clinical research organization with representation from several Canadian-based universities. Each board member of CANMAT has a special clinical, educational, and/or research interest in the area of mood and anxiety disorders and hence brings with him or her a particular strength and expertise.

Child & Adolescent Bipolar Foundation
1000 Skokie Boulevard, Suite 425
Wilmette, IL 60091
http://www.bpkids.org
The Child & Adolescent Bipolar Foundation educates families, professionals, and the public about pediatric bipolar disorder, connects families with resources and support, advocates for and empowers affected families, and supports research on pediatric bipolar disorder and its cure.

Depression and Bipolar Support Alliance
730 North Franklin Street, Suite 501
Chicago, IL 60610
(800) 826-3632
(312) 642-0049
http://www.dbsalliance.org

The Depression and Bipolar Support Alliance (DBSA) is the nation's leading patient-directed organization focusing on the most prevalent mental illnesses—depression and bipolar disorder. The organization fosters an understanding about the impact and management of these life-threatening illnesses by providing up-to-date, scientifically based tools and information written in language the general public can understand. DBSA supports research to promote more timely diagnosis, develop more effective and tolerable treatments, and discover a cure. The organization works to ensure that people living with mood disorders are treated equitably.

Manic Depression Fellowship
Castle Works
21 St. George's Road
London SE1 6ES
United Kingdom
(011) +44 207 793 2600
http://www.mdf.org.uk
MDF The Bipolar Organization is a user-led charity working to enable people affected by bipolar disorder (manic depression) to take control of their lives. The association offers a journal, information about self-help groups, information about the condition, and plenty of advice.

Mood Disorders Society of Canada
3-304 Stone Road West, Suite 763
Guelph, Ontario N1G 4W4
Canada
(519) 824-5565
http://www.mooddisorderscanada.ca
The Mood Disorders Society of Canada is a registered nonprofit organization that is committed to improving quality of life for people affected by depression, bipolar disorder, and other related disorders.

NIMH Mood and Anxiety Disorders Program
NIMH DIRP Scientific Directors Office
10 Center Drive, Room 4N-222, MSC 1381
Bethesda, MD 20892
(866) 627-6464
http://intramural.nimh.nih.gov/mood

The NIMH Mood and Anxiety Disorders Program (MAP) is the world's largest research program focused on mood and anxiety disorders. MAP clinical researchers and basic scientists investigate the diagnosis, treatment, and prevention of serious mood and anxiety disorders. The program is divided into research groups specializing in depression, bipolar disorder, anxiety disorders, post-traumatic stress disorder, and obsessive-compulsive disorder. A broad range of methods are used, including neurochemical, neuroendocrine, neurophysiological, and neuroimaging to conduct studies into the causes and treatment of mood and anxiety disorders.

DEPRESSION

All About Depression
http://www.allaboutdepression.com
This Web site provides accurate, current, and relevant information about clinical depression to the general public. The site includes information about depression, stress, helplessness, discussions, online workshops, helpful books, and much more.

Depressed Anonymous
P.O. Box 17414
Louisville, KY 40217
(502) 569-1989
http://www.depressedanon.com
Depressed Anonymous was formed to provide therapeutic resources for depressed individuals of all ages. DA works with the chronically depressed and those recently discharged from health facilities who were treated for depression. DA also seeks to prevent depression through education and the creation of a supportive and caring community of support groups that successfully keep individuals from relapsing into depression. DA helps prevent depression relapse or recurrence by promoting information and resources helpful for those suffering from depression. DA also works for people who are depressed, including families of those suffering from depression. DA also informs mental health and medical health care professionals about the availability of self-help groups for depressed people.

Depression and Bipolar Support Alliance
730 North Franklin Street, Suite 501
Chicago, IL 60610-7224

(312) 642-0049

http://www.dbsalliance.org

The Depression and Bipolar Support Alliance (DBSA) is the nation's leading patient-directed organization focusing on the most prevalent mental illnesses—depression and bipolar disorder. The organization fosters an understanding about the impact and management of these life-threatening illnesses by providing up-to-date, scientifically based tools and information written in language the general public can understand. DBSA supports research to promote more timely diagnosis, develop more effective and tolerable treatments, and discover a cure. The organization works to ensure that people living with mood disorders are treated equitably.

Depression and Related Affective Disorders Association

2330 West Joppa Road, Suite 100

Lutherville, MD 21093

(410) 583-2919

drada@jhmi.edu

http://www.drada.org

Depression and Related Affective Disorders Association (DRADA) was founded in 1986 by a group of doctors, nurses, and laypersons to provide another form of support to individuals struggling with depression and bipolar illness. In the beginning, this support was provided by mutual-help support groups alone. DRADA has grown significantly since then and now offers many programs, including support groups, accurate information for communities, and educational services. DRADA works in cooperation with the psychiatry department at the Johns Hopkins School of Medicine to ensure that the educational programs and materials produced by the organization reflect accurate and up-to-date information. DRADA receives no funding from Johns Hopkins. Membership dues, program fees, the sales of educational materials, individual gifts, corporate donations, and foundation grants provide funding.

Depression-Guide.com

http://www.depression-guide.com

The Depression Guide Web site provides information for people with depression and is a support resource for family, friends, and loved ones in learning about depression. The site includes the latest information on depression: signs and symptoms, causes, diagnosis, and depression treatment and cure for teens, adults,

*and children. There is also information about coping with the
personal and social effects of depression.*

International Federation for Research and Education on Depression
7040 Bembe Beach Road, Suite 100
Annapolis, MD 21403
(800) 789-2647
http://www.ifred.org
*The International Foundation for Research and Education on
Depression is an action plan based on the desire to find out more
about why clinical depression happens. iFred's mission is to help
support research dedicated to finding solutions to the illness,
to supporting those dealing with depression, and to combating
the stigma associated with it. iFred is an idea spurred by one
woman's struggle with depression and accepting her father's
suicide, with her concern about the significant lack of funding
and education for this treatable condition, and with the public
misunderstanding that fuels the stigma against those trying to
cope with depression.*

Mental Health Research Association
60 Cutter Mill Road, Suite 404
Great Neck, NY 11021
(800) 829-8289
(516) 829-0091
info@narsad.org
http://www.narsad.org
*The Mental Health Research Association (previously known as the
National Alliance for Research on Schizophrenia and Depression)
is the largest donor-supported organization in the world devoted to
funding scientific research on brain and behavior disorders.*

NIMH Mood and Anxiety Disorders Program
NIMH DIRP Scientific Directors Office
10 Center Drive, Room 4N-222, MSC 1381
Bethesda, MD 20892
(866) 627-6464
http://intramural.nimh.nih.gov/mood
*The NIMH Mood and Anxiety Disorders Program (MAP) is the
world's largest research program focused on mood and anxiety
disorders. MAP clinical researchers and basic scientists investigate
the diagnosis, treatment and prevention of serious mood and*

anxiety disorders. The program is divided into research groups specializing in depression, bipolar disorder, anxiety disorders, post-traumatic stress disorder, and obsessive-compulsive disorder. A broad range of methods are used, including neurochemical, neuroendocrine, neurophysiological, and neuroimaging to conduct studies into the causes and treatment of mood and anxiety disorders.

Stress, Anxiety & Depression Resource Center
http://www.stress-anxiety-depression.org/depression
This Web site deals with depression, providing articles, products, books, newsletters, forums, and an e-course.

Students Against Destructive Decisions
255 Main Street
Marlborough, MA 01752
(877) SADD-INC
http://www.sadd.org/contact.htm
Originally, the mission of SADD was to help young people say no to drinking and driving. Today, the mission has expanded because students say positive peer pressure, role models, and other strategies can help them say no to more than drinking and driving. As a result, SADD has become a peer leadership organization dedicated to preventing destructive decisions, particularly underage drinking, other drug use, impaired driving, teen violence, and teen depression and suicide. SADD tries to provide students with the best prevention and intervention tools possible to deal with these destructive decisions.

DIVORCE
Children's Rights Council
6200 Editors Park Drive, Suite 103
Hyattsville, MD 20782
(301) 559-3120
http://www.gocrc.com
Local chapters of the Children's Rights Council throughout the country deal with custody issues and divorce reform.

Divorce Online
NHLBI Information Center
P.O. Box 30105
Bethesda, MD 20824-0105

http://www.divorceonline.com
Divorce Online is for people involved in or facing the prospect of divorce.

Stepfamily Foundation, Inc.
333 West End Avenue
New York, NY 10023
(212) 877-3244
http://www.stepfamily.org
This organization provides phone and in-person counseling and information to create a successful stepfamily relationship. Founded in 1975, the Stepfamily Foundation provides vital training, information, and counseling to avoid the pitfalls that often stress these relationships.

DOMESTIC VIOLENCE
National Coalition Against Domestic Violence
P.O. Box 18749
Denver, CO 80218
(303) 839-1852
http://www.ncadv.org
A national information and referral center for the general public, media, battered women and their children, and allied and member agencies and organizations. NCADV was formally organized in January 1978, when 100 battered women's advocates from all parts of the nation attended the U.S. Commission on Civil Rights hearing on battered women in Washington, D.C., hoping to address common problems these programs often face in isolation. NCADV remains the only national organization of grassroots shelter and service programs for battered women. It is dedicated to the empowerment of battered women and their children and therefore is committed to the elimination of personal and societal violence in their lives.

National CASA (Court Appointed Special Advocate) Association
100 West Harrison–North Tower, Suite 500
Seattle, WA 98119
(800) 628-3233
http://www.nationalcasa.org
National nonprofit organization of trained community volunteers who speak for the best interests of abused and neglected children in court. The group began when a Seattle judge became concerned

*over making decisions about abused and neglected children's
lives without sufficient information; soon judges across the
country began using citizen advocates. In 1990 the U.S. Congress
encouraged the expansion of CASA when it passed the Victims
of Child Abuse Act. Today there are more than 900 CASA
programs, and 62,000 women and men serve as CASA volunteers.
In addition to providing leadership for CASA programs across
the country, the National CASA Association stages an annual
conference, publishes a quarterly newsletter, and promotes CASA
through public relations efforts.*

National Domestic Violence Hotline
P.O. Box 161810
Austin, TX 78716
(800) 799-SAFE (7233)
(800) 787-3224 (TTY)
http://www.ndvh.org
*This hotline was established by the Violence Against Women Act
(VAWA) of 1994; it maintains a database of more than 4,000
shelters and service providers across the United States, Puerto Rico,
Alaska, Hawaii, and the U.S. Virgin Islands. The hotline provides
information and can set up conference calls between battered
women and the nearest shelter. Bilingual staff and a language line
are available for non-English speakers.*

DRUG ABUSE
Co-Anon Family Group
P.O. Box 12722
Tucson, AZ 85732-2722
(800) 898-9985
(520) 513-5028
http://www.co-anon.org
*Co-Anon Family Groups are fellowships of relatives or close friends
of someone who is addicted to cocaine. If you are seeking a
solution to the problems that come from living with a practicing
or recovering cocaine addict, Co-Anon can help you. Members are
relatives and friends who feel their lives have been deeply affected
by another person's drug abuse. Members meet regularly to share
experiences, strength, and hope. By practicing the 12 steps of
recovery, members learn to cope with difficulties and find a more
serene approach to life. Co-Anon has adopted the 12 steps and the
12 traditions of Alcoholics Anonymous. The steps are the heart of*

Co-Anon; the traditions are the backbone. Together, they provide guidelines for personal growth, group harmony, and spiritual enlightenment.

Chemically Dependent Anonymous
General Service Office
P.O. Box 423
Severna Park, MD 21146
(888) CDA-HOPE
http://www.cdaweb.org
CDA is a 12-step fellowship of men and women whose primary purpose is to stay clean and sober and to help others achieve recovery from chemical dependence. CDA deals entirely with the disease of addiction, without making distinctions in the recovery process based on any particular substance, believing that the addictive-compulsive usage of chemicals is the core of the disease and that the use of any mood-changing chemical will result in relapse.

Cocaine Anonymous
3740 Overland Avenue, Suite C
Los Angeles, CA 90034
(310) 559-5833
http://www.ca.org/contact.html
Cocaine Anonymous is a 12-step fellowship of men and women who share their experience, strength, and hope with each other that they may solve their common problem and help others recover from their addiction. The only requirement for membership is a desire to stop using cocaine and all other mind-altering substances. There are no dues or fees for membership, and the group is not allied with any sect, denomination, political party, organization, or institution. Cocaine Anonymous began in Los Angeles in 1982; has since expanded throughout the United States and Canada, and groups are now forming in Europe.

Narcotics Anonymous
P.O. Box 9999
Van Nuys, CA 91409
(818) 773-9999
http://www.na.org
Narcotics Anonymous is an international, community-based association of recovering drug addicts that organizes more than 33,500 weekly meetings in over 116 countries worldwide. It was

developed as a result of the Alcoholics Anonymous program of the late 1940s, and meetings first emerged in the Los Angeles area of California in the early 1950s. The NA program started as a small U.S. movement that has grown into one of the world's oldest and largest organizations of its type.

Nar-Anon
http://www.naranon.com
The Nar-Anon Family Group is primarily for anyone who knows or has known a feeling of desperation concerning the addiction problem of someone very near. The program, which is not a religious one but a spiritual way of life, is based on the 12 suggested steps of Narcotics Anonymous.

National Clearinghouse for Alcohol and Drug Information
P.O. Box 2345
Rockville, MD 20847-2345
(800) 729-6686
(877) 767-8432 (español);
(800) 487-4899 (TTY)
(301) 468-2600
http://www.health.org
The world's largest resource for current information and materials concerning alcohol and substance abuse prevention, intervention, and treatment. NCADI is a service of the Center for Substance Abuse Prevention and offers a wide variety of free services, including NCADI Information Services Department, the NCADI Library, and Prevention Pipeline.

SMART Recovery
7537 Mentor Avenue, Suite 306
Mentor, OH 44060
(866) 951-5357
(440) 951-5357
http://www.smartrecovery.org
SMART Recovery (Self-Management And Recovery Training) helps people recover from all types of addictive behaviors, including alcoholism, drug abuse, substance abuse, drug addiction, alcohol abuse, gambling addiction, cocaine addiction, and addiction to other substances and activities. SMART Recovery is an alternative to Alcoholics Anonymous and Narcotics Anonymous and sponsors more than 300 face-to-face meetings around the world and more than 16 online meetings per week. In addition, its online message

board is an excellent forum in which to learn about SMART Recovery and seek support. SMART Recovery is recognized by the American Academy of Family Physicians, the Center for Health Care Evaluation, the National Institute on Drug Abuse (NIDA), and the American Society of Addiction Medicine.

EATING DISORDERS

National Association of Anorexia Nervosa and Associated Disorders
P.O. Box 7
Highland Park, IL 60035
(847) 831-3438
http://www.anad.org
The oldest national nonprofit organization helping eating disorder victims and their families. In addition to its free hotline counseling, ANAD operates an international network of support groups for sufferers and their families and offers referrals to health care professionals who treat eating disorders across the United States and in many other countries. ANAD publishes a quarterly newsletter and sends information packets customized to individual needs. It also provides speakers, programs, and presentations for schools, colleges, public health agencies, and community groups. It sponsors internships, organizes national conferences and local programs, and works to educate the general public. The association also promotes and develops research projects, fights insurance discrimination and dangerous advertising, and organizes advocacy campaigns to protect potential victims of eating disorders.

National Eating Disorders Association
603 Stewart Street, Suite 803
Seattle, WA 98101
(800) 931-2237
(206) 382-3587
http://www.nationaleatingdisorders.org
Nonprofit organization dedicated to the prevention and treatment of eating disorders. Headquartered in Seattle, Washington, with an office in New York, the National Eating Disorders Association is dedicated to eliminating eating disorders and body dissatisfaction. Through education, advocacy, and research, the association serves as a national authority on eating disorders and related

concerns and as a source for individuals with eating disorders, their loved ones, and their caregivers. It promotes social attitudes that enhance healthy body image and works to overcome the idealization of thinness that contributes to disordered eating.

Overeaters Anonymous
P.O. Box 44020
Rio Rancho, NM 87174-4020
(505) 891-2664
http://www.oa.org
Overeaters Anonymous offers a program of recovery from compulsive overeating using the 12 steps and 12 traditions. Worldwide meetings and other services provide a fellowship of experience, strength, and hope where members respect one another's anonymity. OA charges no dues or fees; it is self-supporting through member contributions. Unlike other organizations, OA is not just about weight loss, obesity, or diets; it addresses physical, emotional, and spiritual well-being. It is not a religious organization and does not promote any particular diet. To address weight loss, OA encourages members to develop a food plan with a health care professional and a sponsor.

FAMILIES
Families for Depression Awareness
300 Fifth Avenue
Waltham, MA 02451
(781) 890-0220
http://www.familyaware.org
Founded in January 2001, Families for Depression Awareness is a nonprofit organization dedicated to helping families recognize and cope with depressive disorders. Families for Depression Awareness helps families, especially family caregivers and friends, recognize and cope with unipolar and bipolar depression. The organization provides education, outreach, and advocacy to support families and friends. Families for Depression Awareness is made up of families who have lost a family member to suicide or have watched a loved one suffer with depression but who have little knowledge about how to help. The group offers brochures such as "Helping Someone Who Is Depressed," educational seminars and outreach training on depression, advocacy to support families with depression, and extensive resources.

Federation of Families for Children's Mental Health
9605 Medical Center Drive, Suite 280
Rockville, MD 20850
(240) 403-1901
ffcmh@ffcmh.com
http://www.ffcmh.org
This national family-run organization is dedicated exclusively to helping children with mental health needs and their families achieve a better quality of life. The group helps policy makers, agencies, and providers become more effective in delivering services and support that foster healthy emotional development for all children.

Research and Training Center on Family Support and Children's Mental Health
Portland State University
P.O. Box 751
Portland, OR 97207-0751
(800) 628-1696
(503) 725-4040 (503) 725-4165 (TTY)
caplane@rri.pdx.edu
http://www.rtc.pdx.edu
This research center is dedicated to promoting effective community-based, culturally competent, family-centered services for families and their children affected by mental, emotional, or behavioral disorders. The center was established in 1984 at Portland State University in Portland, Oregon, with funding from the National Institute on Disability and Rehabilitation Research (NIDRR), the U.S. Department of Education, and the Center for Mental Health Services, Substance Abuse and Mental Health Services Administration, U.S. Department of Health and Human Services. Its goals are accomplished through collaborative research partnerships with family members, service providers, policy makers, and other concerned persons.

Stepfamily Association of America, Inc.
650 J Street, Suite 205
Lincoln, NE 68508
(800) 735-0329
http://www.saafamilies.org
A national nonprofit organization dedicated to providing support and guidance to families with children from previous relationships. SAA provides information, education, support, and advocacy for stepfamilies and those who work with them.

Stepfamily Foundation, Inc.
333 West End Avenue
New York, NY 10023
(212) 877-3244
http://www.stepfamily.org
The Stepfamily Foundation provides counseling on the phone and in person to create a successful stepfamily relationship. Founded in 1975, the Stepfamily Foundation has pioneered this particular method of counseling. It provides vital training, information, and counseling to avoid the pitfalls that often stress these relationships.

FEARS
Freedom From Fear
308 Seaview Avenue
Staten Island, NY 10305
(718) 351-1717 (ext. 24)
help@freedomfromfear.org
http://www.freedomfromfear.org
A national nonprofit mental health advocacy association. The mission of FFF is to improve the lives of all those affected by anxiety, depressive, and related disorders through advocacy, education, research, and community support. The online FFF has developed an anxiety and depression screening program with a free consultation from a health care professional.

GOVERNMENT GROUPS
Center for Mental Health Services
Substance Abuse and Mental Health Services Administration
Room 12-105 Parklawn Building
Rockville, MD 20857
(301) 443-8956
http://www.samhsa.gov
The Substance Abuse and Mental Health Services Administration (SAMHSA), an agency of the U.S. Department of Health and Human Services (HHS), was established by an act of Congress in 1992 under Public Law 102-321. The agency was created to focus attention, programs, and funding on improving the lives of people with or at risk for mental and substance abuse disorders. In collaboration with state, national, and local community-based and faith-based organizations and with public and private sector providers, SAMHSA is working to ensure that people with or

at risk for a mental or addictive disorder have the opportunity for a fulfilling life that includes a job, a home, and meaningful relationships with family and friends.

National Institute of Mental Health
6001 Executive Boulevard, Room 8184, MSC 9663
Bethesda, MD 20892-9663
(866) 615-6464
(301) 443-4513
nimhinfo@nih.gov
http://www.nimh.nih.gov
The National Institute of Mental Health (NIMH) is one of 27 components of the National Institutes of Health, the federal government's principal biomedical and behavioral research agency. The NIMH's mission is to reduce the burden of mental illness and behavioral disorders through research on mind, brain, and behavior. To fulfill its mission, the institute conducts research on mental disorders and the underlying basic science of brain and behavior; supports research at universities and hospitals around the United States; collects, analyzes, and disseminates information on the causes, occurrence, and treatment of mental illnesses; supports the training of more than 1,000 scientists to carry out basic and clinical research; and communicates information to scientists, the public, the news media, and primary care and mental health professionals about mental illnesses, the brain, behavior, mental health, and opportunities and advances in research in these areas.

NIMH Mood and Anxiety Disorders Program
NIMH DIRP Scientific Directors Office
10 Center Drive, Room 4N-222, MSC 1381
Bethesda, MD 20892
(866) 627-6464
http://intramural.nimh.nih.gov/mood/
The NIMH Mood and Anxiety Disorders Program (MAP) is the world's largest research program focused on mood and anxiety disorders. MAP clinical researchers and basic scientists investigate the diagnosis, treatment, and prevention of serious mood and anxiety disorders. The program is divided into research groups specializing in depression, bipolar disorder, anxiety disorders, post-traumatic stress disorder, and obsessive-compulsive disorder. A broad range of methods are used, including neurochemical,

neuroendocrine, neurophysiological, and neuroimaging to conduct studies into the causes and treatment of mood and anxiety disorders.

MENTAL HEALTH
National Mental Health Information Center
P.O. Box 42557
Washington, DC 20015
(800) 789-2647
http://www.mentalhealth.samhsa.gov/
National Mental Health Information Center provides information about mental health through a toll-free telephone number, a Web site, and more than 600 publications. The National Mental Health Information Center was developed for users of mental health services and their families, the general public, policy makers, providers, and the media. Information Center staff members are skilled at listening and responding to questions from the public and professionals. The staff quickly directs callers to federal, state, and local organizations dedicated to treating and preventing mental illness. The Information Center also has information on federal grants and conferences and other events.

OBESITY
American Obesity Association
1250 24th Street NW
Suite 300
Washington, DC 20037
(202) 776-7711
http://www.obesity.org/
The American Obesity Association is the only obesity organization focused on changing public policy and perceptions about obesity. The organization has established an impressive record of changing federal policy, including having the Social Security Administration and the Internal Revenue Service (IRS) recognize obesity as a disease, providing evidence to the IRS to make the costs of obesity treatment eligible for medical deduction, and having Medicare change its policy language on obesity as a disease. The mission of the AOA is to act as an agent of change, move society to rethink obesity as a disease, and fashion appropriate strategies to deal with the epidemic. Currently, obesity is perceived as a failing in an

individual; the association hopes to change that perception to one that recognizes obesity as a complex disease involving more than personal behavior.

International Size Acceptance Association
P.O. Box 82126
Austin, TX 78758
(512) 371-4307
http://www.size-acceptance.org
The mission of the International Size Acceptance Association (ISAA) is to promote size acceptance and fight size discrimination throughout the world. ISAA's primary purpose is to end the most common forms of size discrimination and bigotry against fat children and adults. ISAA defines size discrimination as any action that places people at a disadvantage simply because of their size.

Overeaters Anonymous
P.O. Box 44020
Rio Rancho, NM 87174-4020
(505) 891-2664
http://www.oa.org/index.htm
Overeaters Anonymous offers a program of recovery from compulsive overeating using the 12 steps and 12 traditions. Worldwide meetings and other services provide a fellowship of experience, strength, and hope where members respect one another's anonymity. OA charges no dues or fees; it is self-supporting through member contributions. Unlike other organizations, OA is not just about weight loss, obesity, or diets; it addresses physical, emotional, and spiritual well-being. It is not a religious organization and does not promote any particular diet. To address weight loss, OA encourages members to develop a food plan with a health care professional and a sponsor.

PANIC
The Panic Center
http://www.paniccenter.net
An interactive Web site dedicated to helping those who suffer from panic disorder and to promoting interaction between panic sufferers and health care professionals.

Panic Anxiety Disorder Association
http://www.panicanxietydisorder.org.au

The Panic Anxiety Disorder Association (PADA) is a consumer organization representing people who have a panic or anxiety disorder. Its committee is composed of people who have recovered from an anxiety disorder, plus support people. The association hopes to increase community knowledge and awareness, in addition to providing information and resources to people with anxiety disorders and their support network.

POST-TRAUMATIC STRESS SYNDROME
International Society for Traumatic Stress Studies
60 Revere Drive, Suite 500
Northbrook, IL 60062
(847) 480-9028
istss@istss.org
http://www.istss.org
Nonprofit group dedicated to providing information about studies that seek to reduce traumatic stress and its immediate and long-term consequences. Members of ISTSS include psychiatrists, psychologists, social workers, nurses, counselors, researchers, administrators, advocates, journalists, clergy, and others with an interest in the study and treatment of traumatic stress.

National Center for PTSD
VA Medical Center (116D)
215 North Main Street
White River Junction, VT 05009
(802) 296-6300
http://www.ncptsd.va.gov
The National Center for Post-Traumatic Stress Disorder (PTSD) was created within the Department of Veterans Affairs in 1989, in response to a congressional mandate to address the needs of veterans with military-related PTSD. Its mission is to advance the clinical care and social welfare of America's veterans through research, education, and training in the science, diagnosis, and treatment of PTSD and stress-related disorders.

PTSD Alliance
(877) 507-PTSD
http://www.ptsdalliance.org
A group of professional and advocacy organizations that have joined forces to provide educational resources to individuals diagnosed with PTSD and their loved ones, those at risk for developing PTSD, and medical, health care, and other professionals.

SIDRAN—Sidran Traumatic Stress Foundation
200 E. Joppa Road, Suite 207
Baltimore, MD 21286
(410) 825-8888
http://www.sidran.org
Sidran is a national nonprofit organization devoted to education, advocacy, and research related to the early recognition and treatment of traumatic stress and trauma-generated disorders.

PROFESSIONAL ASSOCIATIONS
American Academy for Child and Adolescent Psychiatry
3615 Wisconsin Avenue NW
Washington, DC 20016
http://www.aacap.org
The AACAP (American Academy of Child and Adolescent Psychiatry) is the leading national professional medical association dedicated to treating these disorders and improving the quality of life for children, adolescents, and families affected by them. The AACAP, a nonprofit organization established in 1953, is composed of more than 7,000 child and adolescent psychiatrists and other interested physicians. Its members actively research, evaluate, diagnose, and treat psychiatric disorders and pride themselves on giving direction to and responding quickly to new developments in addressing the health care needs of children and their families. The AACAP widely distributes information in an effort to promote an understanding of mental illnesses and remove the stigma associated with them, to advance efforts in prevention of mental illnesses, and to ensure proper treatment and access to services for children and adolescents.

American Academy of Pediatrics
141 Northwest Point Boulevard
Elk Grove Village, IL 60007-1098
(847) 434-4000
http://www.aap.org
An organization of more than 60,000 pediatricians committed to attaining optimal physical, mental, and social health and well-being for all infants, children, adolescents, and young adults. The AAP Web site contains general information about children from birth through age 21.

American Group Psychotherapy Association
25 East 21st Street, 6th Floor
New York, NY 10010

(877) 668-2472
(212) 477-2677
http://www.agpa.org

*An association designed for group practitioners in a range of
disciplines who are dedicated to the highest quality and
standards of group therapy. Founded in 1942, AGPA is the
voice of group therapy and other group methods—locally,
nationally, and internationally. Members come from the United
States, Canada, South America, Asia, and Europe and from
12 disciplines, including psychology, creative arts therapy,
psychiatry, nursing, social work, alcoholism counseling, and
marriage and family therapy. The Web site offers a section for
people interested in finding a group therapist and a discussion
of what group therapy is.*

American Psychiatric Association
1000 Wilson Boulevard, Suite 1825
Arlington, VA 22209-3901
(703) 907-7300
http://www.psych.org/index.cfm

*The American Psychiatric Association is a medical specialty society
recognized worldwide. Its more than 35,000 U.S. and international
member physicians work together to ensure humane care and
effective treatment for all persons with mental disorder, including
mental retardation and substance-related disorders. The voice
and conscience of modern psychiatry, it strives to be a society
that provides available, accessible quality psychiatric diagnosis
and treatment. The APA is an organization composed primarily
of medical specialists who are qualified, or in the process
of becoming qualified, as psychiatrists. The basic eligibility
requirement is completion of a residency program in psychiatry
accredited by the Residency Review Committee for Psychiatry
of the Accreditation Council for Graduate Medical Education
(ACGME), the Royal College of Physicians and Surgeons of Canada
(RCPS[C]), or the American Osteopathic Association (AOA).*

American Psychological Association
750 1st Street NE
Washington, DC 20002-4242
(800) 374-2721
(202) 336-5510
http://www.apa.org

*Based in Washington, DC, the American Psychological Association
(APA) is a scientific and professional organization that represents*

psychology in the United States. With 150,000 members, APA is the largest association of psychologists worldwide.

National Mental Health Association
2001 North Beauregard Street, 12th Floor
Alexandria, VA 22311
(800) 969-NMHA
(703) 684-7722
http://www.nmha.org
The National Mental Health Association (NMHA) is the country's oldest and largest nonprofit organization addressing all aspects of mental health and mental illness. With more than 340 affiliates nationwide, NMHA works to improve the mental health of all Americans, especially the 54 million individuals with mental disorders, through advocacy, education, research, and service. NMHA was established in 1909 by former psychiatric patient Clifford W. Beers. During his stays in public and private institutions, Beers witnessed and was subjected to horrible abuse. From these experiences, Beers set into motion a reform movement that took shape as the National Mental Health Association. NMHA's work has resulted in positive change, educating millions about mental illnesses and reduced barriers to treatment and services. As a result, many Americans with mental disorders have sought care and now enjoy fulfilling, productive lives in their communities.

The National Registry of Certified Group Psychotherapists
25 East 21st Street, 6th Floor
New York, NY 10010
(877) 668-2472
(212) 477-2677
http://www.agpa.org
The National Registry of Certified Group Psychotherapists certifies group psychotherapists according to nationally accepted criteria. The registry promotes these practitioners to other mental health professionals, employers, insurers, educators, and clients as maintaining the highest standards for group psychotherapy practice and quality care.

SELF-HELP
Self-Help Group Sourcebook Online
American Self-Help Group Clearinghouse
http://mentalhelp.net/selfhelp

The Self-Help Sourcebook Online is a searchable database that includes information on more than 1,100 national, international, and demonstrational model self-help support groups; ideas for starting groups; and opportunities to link with others to develop needed new national or international groups. This database uses information provided by the American Self-Help Clearinghouse, a department of the Behavioral Health Center of Saint Clare's Health Services in Denville, New Jersey.

Directory of Family Help
http://www.focusas.com/Directory.html
A state-by-state Web site listing of support groups for a wide variety of problems and issues.

Recovery, Inc.
802 North Dearborn Street
Chicago, IL 60610
(312) 337-5661
Recovery, Inc. is a self-help mental health program based on the groundbreaking work of founder Abraham A. Low, M.D. This group is nonprofit, nonsectarian, and completely member managed. Recovery, Inc., has been active since 1937, and groups meet every week around the world.

Students Against Destructive Decisions
255 Main Street
Marlborough, MA 01752
(877) SADD-INC
http://www.sadd.org/contact.htm
Originally, the mission of SADD was to help young people say no to drinking and driving. Today, the mission has expanded because students say positive peer pressure, role models and other strategies can help them say no to more than drinking and driving. As a result, SADD has become a peer leadership organization dedicated to preventing destructive decisions, particularly underage drinking, other drug use, impaired driving, teen violence, and teen depression and suicide. SADD tries to provide students with the best prevention and intervention tools possible to deal with these destructive decisions.

SUICIDE
American Association of Suicidology
4201 Connecticut Avenue NW, Suite 310

Washington, DC 20008
(202) 237-2280
http://www.suicidology.org
The goal of the American Association of Suicidology (AAS) is to
understand and prevent suicide. Founded in 1968 by Edwin S.
Shneidman, Ph.D., AAS promotes research, public awareness
programs, public education, and training for professionals and
volunteers. In addition, AAS serves as a national clearinghouse
for information on suicide. The membership of AAS includes
mental health and public health professionals, researchers, suicide
prevention and crisis intervention centers, school districts, crisis
center volunteers, survivors of suicide, and a variety of laypersons
who have an interest in suicide prevention. AAS, a not-for-profit
organization, encourages and welcomes both individual and
organizational members.

American Foundation for Suicide Prevention
120 Wall Street, 22nd Floor
New York, NY 10005
(888) 333-AFSP
(212) 363-3500
http://www.afsp.org/index-1.htm
The American Foundation for Suicide Prevention (AFSP) is the
only national not-for-profit organization exclusively dedicated
to funding research, developing prevention initiatives, and
offering educational programs and conferences for survivors,
mental health professionals, physicians, and the public. The
foundation's activities include supporting research projects that
further the understanding and treatment of depression and the
prevention of suicide; providing information and education about
depression and suicide; promoting professional education for the
recognition and treatment of depressed and suicidal individuals;
publicizing the magnitude of the problems of depression and
suicide and the need for research, prevention, and treatment;
and supporting programs for suicide survivor treatment, research,
and education.

notMYkid.org
33 West Indian School Road
Phoenix, AZ 85013-3205
(602) 652-0163
http://www.notmykid.org

*A national nonprofit organization devoted to educating individuals
and communities about behavioral health issues facing teens
today, believing that education leads to prevention.*

Students Against Destructive Decisions
255 Main Street
Marlborough, MA 01752
(877) SADD-INC
http://www.sadd.org/contact.htm
*Originally, the mission of SADD was to help young people say
no to drinking and driving. Today, the mission has expanded
because students say positive peer pressure, role models and
other strategies can help them say no to more than drinking
and driving. As a result, SADD has become a peer leadership
organization dedicated to preventing destructive decisions,
particularly underage drinking, other drug use, impaired driving,
teen violence, and teen depression and suicide. SADD tries to
provide students with the best prevention and intervention tools
possible to deal with these destructive decisions.*

Suicide Prevention Action Network
1025 Vermont Avenue, NW, Suite 1066
Washington, DC 20005
(202) 449-3600
http://www.spanusa.org
*The Suicide Prevention Action Network (SPAN USA) is dedicated
to preventing suicide through public education and awareness,
community action, and federal, state, and local grassroots
advocacy. The organization was founded in 1996 by Gerald
and Elsie Weyrauch of Marietta, Georgia, whose 34-year-old
physician daughter, Terri, committed suicide. Their goal was to
create a way for the loved ones of suicide victims to transform
their grief into positive action to prevent future tragedies. SPAN
USA's members are people in communities across the country,
including family members and friends of suicide victims,
people who have attempted suicide or struggled with suicidal
thoughts and their families, professionals serving families and
communities, community leaders, and concerned citizens. SPAN
USA is the nation's only suicide prevention organization dedicated
to leveraging grassroots support among suicide survivors and
others to advance public policies that help prevent suicide. The
organization was created to raise awareness, build political*

will, and call for action with regard to creating, advancing, implementing, and evaluating a national strategy to address suicide in the United States. Since the organization was founded, grassroots volunteers and staff have worked in communities, state capitols, and Washington, D.C., to advance a public policy response to the problem of suicide in America.

Yellow Ribbon International
P.O. Box 644
Westminster, CO 80036-0644
(303) 429-3530
ask4help@yellowribbon.org
http://www.yellowribbon.org
Yellow Ribbon is a community-based nonprofit program using a universal public health approach to empower and educate professionals, adults, and youths about suicide.

TREATMENT
The Association for Behavioral and Cognitive Therapies
305 7th Avenue, 16th floor
New York, NY 10001
(212) 647-1890
http://www.aabt.org
The Association for the Advancement of Behavior Therapy is a professional interdisciplinary organization that is concerned with applying behavioral and cognitive sciences to understanding human behavior, developing interventions to enhance the human condition, and promoting the appropriate use of these interventions.

Academy of Cognitive Therapy
One Belmont Avenue, Suite 700
Bala Cynwyd, PA 19004-1610
(610) 664-1273
(610) 664-5137 (fax)
http://www.academyofct.org
The Academy of Cognitive Therapy is the only certifying organization for cognitive-behavioral therapy that evaluates applicants' knowledge and ability before granting certification. The standards of the academy are designed to identify clinicians with the necessary training, experience, and knowledge to be effective cognitive therapists. Lack of rigor in certification represents a

significant problem for both clinicians and clients. Certification by the Academy of Cognitive Therapy indicates to the public, potential employers, and other clinicians that the individual is a skilled cognitive therapist. The board, officers, and founding fellows of the academy are highly experienced cognitive-behavioral therapists who have made major contributions to the development of this treatment approach. They have designed the certification process to identify therapists who are expert clinicians.

The International Association for Cognitive Psychotherapy (IACP)
http://www.cognitivetherapyassociation.org
The IACP is a professional, scientific, interdisciplinary organization whose mission is to encourage the growth of cognitive psychotherapy as a professional activity and scientific discipline. In addition, the association serves as a resource and information center for matters related to cognitive psychotherapy. The honorary president of the association is Aaron T. Beck, MD, University Professor Emeritus of psychiatry at the University of Pennsylvania, and president of the Beck Institute for Cognitive Therapy and Research in suburban Philadelphia.

APPENDIX 2

Drug Company
Patient Assistance Programs

LISTED BY DRUG

Anafranil
Pharmacy Providers of Oklahoma
P.O. Box 18204
Oklahoma City, OK 73154
http://www.ppok.com
(800) 259-7765

BuSpar
Bristol-Myers Squibb Patient Assistance Foundation Inc.
P.O. Box 2118
Lakewood, NJ 08701-9846
(800) 736-0003

Desyrel (150- and 300-mg pills only)
Bristol-Myers Squibb Company
(800) 332-2056

Effexor, Effexor SR
Wyeth-Ayerst Laboratories
Patient Assistance Program
P.O. Box 13806
Philadelphia, PA 19101
(800) 568-9938

Elavil
Zeneca Pharmaceuticals
(800) 424-3727

Klonopin
Roche Laboratories, Inc.
Roche Medical Needs Program
Medical Needs
340 Kingsland Street
Nutley, NJ 07110
(800) 285-4484

Lithium (Eskalith CR)
SmithKline Pharmaceuticals, Inc.
SmithKline Beecham Foundation Access to Care
c/o Express Scripts/SDS
P.O. Box 2564
Maryland Heights, MO 63043-8564
(800) 546-0420
(800) 729-4544

Lithium (Lithobid)
Solvay Pharmaceuticals, Inc.
Solvay Patient Assistance Program
c/o Express Scripts Specialty Distribution Service
P.O. Box 66550
St. Louis, MO 63166-6550
(800) 256-8918
http://www.solvaypharmaceuticals-us.com/patients/
    patientassistanceprogram/0,998, 7438-2-0,00.htm

Loxitane
Lederle Laboratories
(703) 706-5933

Ludiomil
Ciba Pharmaceuticals
(800) 257-3273

Luvox
Solvay Pharmaceuticals, Inc.
(800) 788-9277

Navane
Pfizer Inc.
Connection to Care
P.O. Box 66585

St. Louis, MO 63166-6585
(800) 707-8990
https://www.pfizerhelpfulanswers.com/ProgramList.aspx

Norpramin
Hoechst Marion Roussel, Inc.
(800) 221-4025

Parnate
SmithKline Pharmaceuticals, Inc.
SmithKline Beecham Foundation Access to Care
c/o Express Scripts/SDS
P.O. Box 2564
Maryland Heights, MO 63043-8564
(800) 546-0420
(800) 729-4544

Paxil, Paxil CR
SmithKline Pharmaceuticals, Inc.
SmithKline Beecham Foundation Access to Care
c/o Express Scripts/SDS
P.O. Box 2564
Maryland Heights, MO 63043-8564
(800) 546-0420
(800) 729-4544

Prozac
Eli Lilly and Company
Lilly Cares
P.O. Box 230999
Centerville, VA 20120
(800) 545-6962
http://www.lilly.com/products/access/direct_patient.html

Remeron
Organon Inc.
Remeron SolTab Patient Assistance Program
375 Mount Pleasant Avenue
West Orange, NJ 07052
(800) 631-1253

Risperdal
Janssen Pharmaceutical
Risperdal Patient Assistance and Reimbursement Support Program

P.O. Box 222098
Charlotte, NC 28222-2098
(800) 652-6227

Serax
Wyeth-Ayerst Laboratories
(703) 706-5933

Serentil
Boehringer Ingelheim Pharmaceuticals, Inc.
(800) 556-8317

Seroquel
AstraZeneca Pharmaceuticals Patient Assistance Program Foundation
P.O. Box 15197
Wilmington, DE 19850-5197
(800) 424-3727
http://www.astrazeneca-us.com/content/drugAssistance/
   patientAssistanceProgram/d efault.asp

Serzone
Bristol-Myers Squibb Patient Assistance Foundation Inc.
P.O. Box 2118
Lakewood, NJ 08701-9846
(800) 736-0003

Sinequan
Pfizer Inc.
Connection to Care
P.O. Box 66585
St. Louis, MO 63166-6585
(800) 707-8990
https://www.pfizerhelpfulanswers.com/ProgramList.aspx

Tegretol, Tegretol-XR
Novartis Pharmaceuticals
Novartis Patient Assistance Program
P.O. Box 66556
St. Louis, MO 63166-6556
(800) 277-2254
http://www.pharma.us.novartis.com/novartis/pap/pap.
   jsp?checked = y

Topamax
Ortho-McNeil Pharmaceutical
Ortho-McNeil Patient Assistance Program
1250 Bayhill Drive
Suite 300
San Bruno, CA 94066
http://www.ortho-mcneilneurologics.com/html/comn/company_
assistance.jsp

Valium
Roche Laboratories, Inc.
Roche Medical Needs Program
Medical Needs
340 Kingsland Street
Nutley, NJ 07110
(800) 285-4484

Wellbutrin, Wellbutrin SR
GlaxoSmithKline Inc.
Bridges to Access
P.O. Box 29038
Phoenix, AZ 85038
(866) 728-4368
http://www.bridgestoaccess.com

Zoloft
Pfizer Inc.
Connection to Care
P.O. Box 66585
St. Louis, MO 63166-6585
(800) 707-8990
https://www.pfizerhelpfulanswers.com/ProgramList.aspx

Zyprexa
Eli Lilly and Company
LillyCares: Zyprexa Patient Assistance Program
P.O. Box 231000
Centerville, VA 20120
(800) 488-2133
http://www.lilly.com/products/access/direct_patient.html

GLOSSARY

affective disorder   A term that includes all mood disorders, including depression and bipolar depression.

agitated depression   A major depressive disorder featuring insomnia, restlessness, and appetite loss.

alprazolam (Xanax)   A benzodiazepine tranquilizer used to treat anxiety and panic disorder.

amitriptyline (Elavil)   A tricyclic antidepressant.

amoxapine (Asendin)   A tricyclic antidepressant.

amygdala   A small region of the brain that experts believe is very important in the fear response, in emotions, and in anxiety.

Anafranil   See CLOMIPRAMINE.

anhedonia   The inability to experience pleasure from activities that once brought pleasure.

anticholinergic effects   A group of common side effects caused by the interference with the action of acetylcholine in the brain and peripheral nervous system. These side effects are most typically caused by tricyclic antidepressants, including dry mouth, constipation, urination problems, and blurry vision.

antidepressant   A medication used to treat depression and sometimes to treat anxiety disorders as well. Antidepressants include the modern, commonly used medications called selective serotonin reuptake inhibitors (SSRIs), plus tricyclic antidepressants and monoamine oxidase inhibitors (MAOIs).

anxiolytic   Antianxiety medication.

Ativan   See LORAZEPAM.

atypical bipolar II depression   A clinical condition in which a person experiences periods of major depression alternating with periods of mild elation.

atypical depression   A type of depression in which the person may gain weight, sleep more than usual, and react to the environment. This condition is the opposite of typical depression, which is characterized by weight loss and insomnia.

automatic thoughts   Thoughts or beliefs about everyday activities that occur so quickly that the person almost does not consciously recognize them. In cognitive therapy, clients are taught to try to reduce or eliminate automatic thoughts with cognitive distortions.

Aventyl   See NORTRIPTYLINE.

aversion therapy   A type of behavior therapy in which punishment or negative stimulation is used to eliminate undesired responses.

barbiturate   A habit-forming medication used to treat anxiety or induce sleep.

behavior modification   Techniques based on learning theory that are used to change a person's behavior by applying positive and negative reinforcement to increase the occurrence of desirable behaviors.

behavior therapy   A type of psychotherapy treatment used to help patients gain control of depression by substituting healthy responses and behavior patterns for unhealthy ones by using exposure and relaxation techniques.

benzodiazepines   A class of hypnotic sedative drugs that act as tranquilizers, which may be used to treat some symptoms of some anxiety disorders. They are also used as a sleeping aid for insomnia.

beta blockers   A class of drugs typically used to lower blood pressure that also may be prescribed to ease physical symptoms of anxiety associated with social phobia and some other anxiety disorders.

biofeedback   A therapy technique in which a person is taught to control body processes not normally considered to be under voluntary control, such as heart rate or skin temperature.

biogenic amines   Organic substances that include catecholamines (epinephrine, dopamine, and norepinephrine) and indoles (tryptophan and serotonin), all of which may play a role in the development of depression.

bipolar disorder   A major affective disorder characterized by both mania and depression (once known as manic depression). Bipolar disorder may be divided into manic, depressed, or mixed types based on the person's symptoms.

bipolar disorder, depressed type   A type of bipolar disorder characterized by low mood, slowed thinking, loss of interest, guilt, negative self-esteem, appetite loss, and sleep problems.

bipolar disorder, manic type   A type of bipolar disorder that causes excitement and euphoria, hyperactivity, pressured speech, flight of ideas, insomnia, distractibility, and impaired judgment. There may be elated delusions of grandiose abilities.

bipolar disorder, mixed type   A type of bipolar disorder characterized by symptoms of both mania and depression that occur at the same time.

bipolar I disorder   A clinical condition characterized by alternating episodes of major depression and mania, or elation, that often requires hospitalization.

bipolar II disorder   A clinical condition characterized by alternating periods of major depression and mild mania that may require hospitalization during the depressed phase, but not usually during the manic phase.

bipolar III disorder   A term used to describe a depressed person with only mild or severe mania (not depression) that develops after taking certain drugs, such as antidepressants.

brief psychotherapy   Short-term therapy of eight to 12 sessions.

bupropion (Wellbutrin)   An antidepressant.

BuSpar   See BUSPIRONE.

buspirone (BuSpar)   A non–habit-forming antianxiety medication.

carbamazepine (Tegretol)   An anticonvulsant medication used as an alternative to lithium in the treatment of bipolar disorder.

Celexa   See CITALOPRAM.

chlordiazepoxide (Librium)   An antianxiety drug that belongs to the benzodiazepine family.

cholinergic   A term that means "activated by acetylcholine."

citalopram (Celexa)   An antidepressant of the selective serotonin reuptake inhibitor (SSRI) class.

clinical depression   A medical term used interchangeably with the term *major depression.*

clomipramine (Anafranil)   A tricyclic antidepressant used to treat depression and obsessive-compulsive disorder.

cognition   Knowing, thinking, or perceiving.

cognitive-behavioral perspective   A theoretical approach to understanding behavior that focuses on how a person's thoughts and behavior are related to each other and how thoughts can become distorted to contribute to problem behavior.

cognitive-behavioral therapy (CBT)   A type of therapy focusing on specific cognitive and behavioral therapy techniques used to change thoughts and behavior.

cognitive restructuring   A cognitive technique in which distorted thoughts or beliefs are evaluated and alternative beliefs are substituted for them.

cognitive therapy   A form of psychotherapy based on the idea that emotional disorders are affected by distorted thought patterns and core beliefs that can be changed.

coping strategies   Techniques that people use to cope with stress.

cyclothymia   A form of bipolar disorder characterized by mild highs and lows.

Depakote   See VALPROIC ACID.

depressive reaction   A sense of despondency and distress that is a normal, healthy response to a significant loss or a stressful situation. This type of reaction is usually comparatively mild to moderate and usually improves within two weeks to six months.

desipramine (Norpramin)   A tricyclic antidepressant.

Desyrel   See TRAZODONE.

diazepam (Valium)   An antianxiety medication and minor tranquilizer.

dopamine A chemical neurotransmitter in the brain that, at low levels, is associated with depression.

double depression A episode of major depression that occurs at the same time as a chronic, long-term milder depression.

DSM-IV-TR *Diagnostic and Statistical Manual of Mental Disorders*, 4th ed. (Text Revision). An American Psychiatric Association publication that lists all symptoms for all psychiatric disorders.

dysphoria The opposite of euphoria, in which a person feels emotional or mentally uncomfortable, with restlessness, malaise, and depression. Dysphoria is different from simple depression in that it tends to include agitated feelings. People with bipolar disorder experience dysphoric highs.

dysthymic disorder A mild but persistent form of depression (also called depressive neurosis) that lasts for at least one year in children. Other symptoms include loss of appetite or overeating, insomnia or excessive sleepiness, poor self-esteem, inability to concentrate, low energy, and feelings of hopelessness.

Effexor See VENLAFAXINE.

Elavil See AMITRIPTYLINE.

endogenous depression A seemingly unprovoked, unexplained, spontaneous feeling of depression that may be moderate to severe.

environmental stressors Situations or events in the environment, such as work, school, crowds, relationships, or noise, that cause stress.

epinephrine (adrenaline) A hormone and neurotransmitter secreted by the adrenal gland during periods of stress that triggers a variety of changes in the body, including a rise in blood sugar and blood pressure. High levels of epinephrine have been associated with feelings of fear and anxiety and with panic attacks.

family therapy A type of treatment in which a patient and his or her family is treated together.

flight of ideas Switching a topic midsentence or inappropriately or "racing thoughts."

fluoxetine (Prozac) The first selective serotonin reuptake inhibitor (SSRI) antidepressant.

fluvoxamine (Luvox) A selective serotonin reuptake inhibitor (SSRI) antidepressant.

generic drug A term that refers to the chemical name of a drug, not its brand or trade name. For example, fluoxetine is the generic term for Prozac. Names of generic drugs are never capitalized.

hyperthymia A mood of high energy and confidence that is considered to be more energetic than normal but not so active as a mild form of mania.

hypomania A mildly elevated mood that is less intense than mania but more intense than hyperthymia.

imipramine (Tofranil) A tricyclic antidepressant.

interpersonal psychotherapy A type of short-term psychotherapy used to treat depression.

Lamictal See LAMOTRIGINE.

lamotrigine (Lamictal) An anticonvulsant medication that can stabilize mood and that is used to treat resistant bipolar disorder.

Librium See CHLORDIAZEPOXIDE.

lithium An element used as a medication to treat bipolar disorder, valued for its ability to stabilize the fluctuating manic and depressive moods.

lorazepam (Ativan) An antianxiety medication that is also prescribed for people experiencing both anxiety and depression.

L-tryptophan An amino acid used by the body to produce serotonin.

Ludiomil See MAPROTILINE.

Luvox See FLUVOXAMINE.

major affective disorder A group of disorders characterized by a persistent, prominent disturbed mood (such as mania or depression). Major depression and bipolar disorder are both examples of a major affective disorder.

major depressive disorder A mood disorder characterized by the occurrence of one or more major depressive episodes, without any history of manic, mixed, or mild manic episodes.

major depressive episode A depressive episode (also known as clinical depression or unipolar depression) that lasts at least two weeks and is characterized by feelings of sadness, worthlessness, or guilt; loss of ability to experience pleasure; fatigue; appetite and sleep problems; concentration problems; and frequent suicidal thoughts. If at least four of these symptoms occur in addition to at least one episode of mania, the diagnosis is bipolar disorder.

mania An episode of elation and high mood that may be characterized by hyperactivity, rapid talking, agitation, excitement, and flight of ideas.

manic depression The former term for bipolar disorder.

MAO See MONOAMINE OXIDASE.

MAOI See MONOAMINE OXIDASE INHIBITOR.

maprotiline (Ludiomil) A tetracyclic antidepressant.

masked depression Depression that is hidden beneath physical symptoms that have no apparent physical cause.

melancholia A severe form of depression. *Major depression with melancholia* is a term used to describe a severe depression involving loss of pleasure, agitation, bad morning mood, weight loss, and insomnia.

metabolite A chemical compound that is produced when a drug is broken down in the body.

mirtazapine (Remeron) An atypical antidepressant that prevents neurotransmitters from binding with nerve cell receptors called alpha-2 receptors, raising the levels of norepinephrine and serotonin in the brain.

monoamine oxidase (MAO) An enzyme that breaks down neurotransmitters (biogenic amines). Certain antidepressants (MAO inhibitors) interfere with this enzyme, which may relieve a person's depression.

monoamine oxidase inhibitor (MAOI) A class of antidepressants that prevents the enzyme monoamine oxidase from breaking down, which leads to higher levels of norepinephrine and serotonin in the brain.

mood disorders A group of conditions characterized by a lack of control over emotions and mood. Mood disorders such as depression and mania can interfere with a person's appetite, sleep patterns, thinking ability, and mood and can seriously affect a person's personal life at every level.

Nardil   See PHENELZINE.

nefazodone (Serzone)   The first of a new type of atypical antidepressants that combined the mechanism of an SSRI and a tricyclic, inhibiting the reuptake of neurotransmitters into nerve cells and blocking nerve cell receptors. This leaves more mood-related brain chemicals available in the brain, thereby boosting mood.

negative automatic thoughts   Negative thoughts about oneself and the future that occur automatically and unconsciously.

neuron   A nerve cell.

neurosis   A disorder characterized by anxiety or exaggerated avoidance of anxiety. The person who is neurotic understands that this behavior is not normal.

neurotransmitter   A chemical substance released by nerve cell endings that transmits information across the gaps (synapses) between nerve cells. Problems with the neurotransmitters, such as abnormally low levels, have been linked to depression. Serotonin, norepinephrine, and dopamine are all examples of neurotransmitters.

norepinephrine (noradrenaline)   A hormone and neurotransmitter produced by the adrenal gland. High levels of this chemical have been linked to mania; low levels have been linked to depression.

Norpramin   See DESIPRAMINE.

nortriptyline (Aventyl, Pamelor)   A tricyclic antidepressant.

orthostatic hypotension   A sudden drop in blood pressure when a person suddenly stands up, causing dizziness or fainting. This is a common side effect of some antidepressants.

Pamelor   See NORTRIPTYLINE.

Parnate   See TRANYLCYPROMINE.

paroxetine (Paxil)   An SSRI antidepressant.

Paxil   See PAROXETINE.

phenelzine (Nardil) An MAOI antidepressant.

progressive muscle relaxation A method of relaxation in which individual muscle groups are systematically tensed and relaxed that can be used to ease symptoms of anxiety.

protriptyline (Vivactil) A tricyclic antidepressant.

Prozac See FLUOXETINE.

psychotropic drug A medication that affects mood or mental activity.

rapid cycler A person with bipolar disorder who experiences more than four mood swings a year.

rebound The return of symptoms after treatment ends.

relaxation technique Techniques such as breathing exercises, meditation, and yoga that are used to relax and ease symptoms of anxiety.

Remeron See MIRTAZAPINE.

selective serotonin reuptake inhibitor (SSRI) A class of antidepressants used to treat some types of anxiety disorders that work by boosting the amount of serotonin in the brain.

serotonin A brain chemical (neurotransmitter) linked to mood. Low levels of serotonin in the brain are believed to trigger symptoms of depressed mood, anxiety, panic, or obsessions and compulsions.

serotonin and norepinephrine reuptake inhibitor (SNRI) A group of antidepressants believed to affect two naturally occurring chemicals in the brain (serotonin and norepinephrine), both of which are responsible for controlling mood and emotion. SNRIs include Effexor (venlafaxine) and Cymbalta (duloxetine).

sertraline (Zoloft) An SSRI antidepressant.

Serzone See NEFAZODONE.

SNRI See SEROTONIN and NOREPINEPHRINE REUPTAKE INHIBITOR.

soft bipolar A very mild type of mania that is too mild to meet the requirements of a formal diagnosis.

SSRI See SELECTIVE SEROTONIN REUPTAKE INHIBITOR.

stressor A situation or thought that causes stress.

subclincal depression   A type of depression that is not severe enough to meet the criteria for a diagnosis of major depression or dysthymia.

Surmontil   See TRIMIPRAMINE.

synapse   The gap between two neurons where the transmission of nerve impulses occurs.

Tegretol   See CARBAMAZEPINE.

tetracyclic antidepressant   A type of antidepressant named for its four-ring chemical structure. Ludiomil is an example of a tetracyclic.

Tofranil   See IMIPRAMINE.

Topamax   See TOPIRAMATE.

topiramate (Topamax)   A mood-stabilizing anticonvulsant drug used to treat bipolar disorder.

tranylcypromine (Parnate)   An MAOI antidepressant.

trazodone (Desyrel)   An atypical antidepressant that is structurally unlike the tricyclics, MAOIs, or selective serotonin reuptake inhibitors (SSRIs).

treatment-resistant depression   A depression that is not improved by any of the major classes of antidepressants.

tricyclic antidepressant (TCA)   A class of antidepressants that may be used to treat some anxiety disorders, thought to work by regulating several neurotransmitters, including norepinephrine and serotonin. It is named for its three-ring chemical structure.

trimipramine (Surmontil)   A tricyclic antidepressant.

Valium   See DIAZEPAM.

valproic acid (Depakote)   An anticonvulsant medication used as an alternative for lithium in the treatment of bipolar disorder.

venlafaxine (Effexor)   A selective norepinephrine reuptake inhibitor (SNRI) antidepressant.

Vivactil   See PROTRIPTYLINE.

Wellbutrin   See BUPROPRION.

withdrawal symptoms Symptoms such as tremor, sweating, vomiting, insomnia, muscle pain, anxiety, or convulsions that occur after a drug that causes physical dependence is suddenly stopped.

Xanax See ALPRAZOLAM.

Zoloft See SERTRALINE.

READ MORE ABOUT IT

BIPOLAR DISORDER

Birmaher, Boris. *New Hope for Children and Teens with Bipolar Disorder: Your Friendly, Authoritative Guide to the Latest in Traditional and Complementary Solutions.* New York: Three Rivers Press, 2004.

Carlson, Trudy. *Life of a Bipolar Child: What Every Parent and Professional Needs to Know.* Duluth, Minn.: Benline Press, 2000.

Evans, Dwight, and Linda Wasmer Andrews. *If Your Adolescent Has Depression or Bipolar Disorder: An Essential Resource for Parents.* New York: Oxford University Press, 2005.

Lynn, George. *Survival Strategies for Parenting Children with Bipolar Disorder: Innovative Parenting and Counseling Techniques for Helping Children with Bipolar Disorder and the Conditions That May Occur with It.* London: Jessica Kingsley Publishing, 2000.

Papolos, Demitri F. *The Bipolar Child: The Definitive and Reassuring Guide to Childhood's Most Misunderstood Disorder.* New York: Broadway Books, 2000.

Peacock, Judith. *Bipolar Disorder.* Santa Rosa, Calif.: LifeMatters, 2000.

Waltz, Mitzi. *Bipolar Disorders: A Guide to Helping Children and Adolescents.* Sebastopol, Calif.: Patient Centered Guides, 2000.

DEPRESSION

Burns, David D. *The Feeling Good Handbook.* New York: Plume, 1999.

Carlson, Trudy. *Depression in the Young: What We Can Do to Help Them.* Duluth, Minn.: Benline Press, 1998

Carter, Sharon, and Lawrence Clayton. *Coping with Depression.* Twin Cities, Minn.: Hazelden, 1997.

Cobain, Bev. *When Nothing Matters Anymore: A Survival Guide for Depressed Teens.* Minneapolis: Free Spirit Publishing, 1998.

Crist, James. *What to Do When You're Sad and Lonely: A Guide for Kids.* Minneapolis: Free Spirit Publishing, 2005.

Depaulo, Raymond, Jr. *How to Cope with Depression.* New York: Ballantine, 1996.

Empfield, Maureen, and Nick Bakalar. *Understanding Teenage Depression: A Guide to Diagnosis, Treatment, and Management.* New York: Owl Books, 2001.

Evans, Dwight, and Linda Wasmer Andrews. *If Your Adolescent Has Depression or Bipolar Disorder: An Essential Resource for Parents.* New York: Oxford University Press, 2005.

Faraone, Stephen. *Straight Talk about Your Child's Mental Health: What to Do When Something Seems Wrong.* New York: Guilford Press, 2003.

Fassler, David G. *Help Me, I'm Sad: Recognizing, Treating, and Preventing Childhood and Adolescent Depression.* New York: Penguin Books, 1998.

Garland, E. Jane. *Depression Is the Pits, but I'm Getting Better: A Guide for Adolescents* Washington, D.C.: Magination Press, 1998.

Golant, Mitch, and Susan K. Golant. *What to Do When Someone You Love Is Depressed: A Practical, Compassionate, and Helpful Guide for Caregivers.* New York: Owl Books, 1998.

Greenberger, Dennis, and Christine Padesky. *Mind over Mood: Change How You Feel by Changing the Way You Think.* New York: Guilford Press, 1995.

Hicks, James. *Fifty Signs of Mental Illness: A Guide to Understanding Mental Health.* New Haven: Yale University Press, 2005.

Ingersoll, Barbara D. *Lonely, Sad, and Angry: A Parent's Guide to Depression in Children and Adolescents.* New York: Main Street Books, 1996.

Irwin, Cait. *Conquering the Beast Within: How I Fought Depression and Won . . . and How You Can, Too.* New York: Three Rivers Press, 1999.

Kaufman, Miriam. *Overcoming Teen Depression: A Guide for Parents.* Issues in Parenting. New York: Firefly Books, 2001.

Klebanoff, Susan. *Ups and Downs: How to Beat the Blues and Teen Depression.* Los Angeles: Price Stern Sloan, 1998.

Koplewicz, Harold S. *More Than Moody: Recognizing and Treating Adolescent Depression.* New York: Perigee Books, 2003.

Lewinsohn, Peter, et al. *Control Your Depression.* New York: Fireside, 1992.

Manassis, Katharina, and Anne Marie Levac. *Helping Your Teenager Beat Depression: A Problem-Solving Approach for Families.* Winston-Salem, N.C.: Woodbine House, 2004.

Miller, Jeffrey A. *The Childhood Depression Sourcebook.* Los Angeles: Lowell House, 1998.

Mondimore, Francis. *Adolescent Depression: A Guide for Parents.* Baltimore: Johns Hopkins Press, 2002.

O'Connor, Richard. *Undoing Depression.* New York: Berkley Trade, 1999.

Oster, Gerald, and Sarah S. Montgomery. *Helping Your Depressed Teen-ager: A Guide for Parents and Caregivers.* New York: Wiley, 1994.

Potts, Kimberly. *What's Your Mood? A Good Day / Bad Day / In-Between Day Book.* Cincinnatti: Adams Media Corp, 2004.

Quinn, Brian. *The Depression Sourcebook.* New York: Contemporary Books, 1998.

Rosen, Laura, and Xavier Francisco Amador. *When Someone You Love Is Depressed: How to Help Your Loved One without Losing Yourself.* New York: Fireside Press, 1997.

Seligman, Martin E. *The Optimistic Child: Proven Program to Safeguard Children from Depression and Build Lifelong Resilience.* New York: Harper, 1996.

Sheffield, Anne, and Donald F. Klein. *How You Can Survive When They're Depressed: Living and Coping with Depression Fallout.* New York: Three Rivers Press, 1999.

Silverstein, Alvin. *Depression.* Berkeley Heights, N.J.: Enslow Publishers, 1997.

Strauss, Claudia. *Talking to Depression: Simple Ways to Connect When Someone in Your Life Is Depressed.* New York: New American Library, 2004.

Yapko, Michael D. *Breaking the Patterns of Depression.* New York: Main Street Books, 1998.

———. *Hand-Me-Down Blues.* New York: St. Martin's Press, 2000.

———. *When Living Hurts: Directives for Treating Depression.* Levittown, Pa.: Brunner/Mazel.

EATING DISORDERS

Costin, Carolyn. *The Eating Disorder Sourcebook: A Comprehensive Guide to the Causes, Treatments, and Prevention of Eating Disorders.* New York: McGraw-Hill, 1999.

Siegel, Michelle. *Surviving an Eating Disorder.* New York: HarperCollins, 1997.

PANIC

Antony, Martin M., and Randi McCabe. *10 Simple Solutions to Panic: How to Overcome Panic Attacks, Calm Physical Symptoms, and Reclaim Your Life.* Oakland, Calif.: New Harbinger, 2004.

Babior, Shirley, and Carol Goldman. *Overcoming Panic, Anxiety, and Phobias: New Strategies to Free Yourself from Worry and Fear.* Duluth, Minn.: Whole Person Associates, 1996.

Bassett, Lucinda. *From Panic to Power: Proven Techniques to Calm Your Anxieties, Conquer Your Fears, and Put You in Control of Your Life.* New York: HarperResource, 1997.

Bemis, Judith. *Embracing the Fear: Learning to Manage Anxiety and Panic Attacks.* Twin Cities, Minn.: Hazelden, 1994.

Carbonell, David. *Panic Attacks Workbook: A Guided Program for Beating the Panic Trick.* Berkeley: Ulysses Press, 2004.

Dumont, Raeann. *The Sky Is Falling: Understanding and Coping with Phobias, Panic, and Obsessive-Compulsive Disorders.* New York: W. W. Norton, 1997.

Granoff, Abbot Lee. *Help! I Think I'm Dying! Panic Attacks and Phobias: A Consumer's Guide.* Norfolk, Va.: Mind Matters, 1999.

Peurifoy, Reneau Z. *Anxiety, Phobias, and Panic: A Step-by-Step Program for Regaining Control of Your Life.* Rev. ed. New York: Warner Books, 2005.

Silove, Derrick. *Overcoming Panic: A Self-Help Guide Using Cognitive Behavioral Techniques.* New York: New York University Press, 2001.

Wiederhold, Brenda K. *Conquering Panic, Anxiety, and Phobias: Achieving Success through Virtual Reality and Cognitive-Behavioral Therapy.* San Diego: Virtual Reality Medical Center Publications, 2004.

Wilson, R. Reid. *Don't Panic, Revised Edition: Taking Control of Anxiety Attacks.* New York: Collins, 1996.

POST-TRAUMATIC STRESS DISORDER

Fitzgerald, Helen. *The Grieving Teen: A Guide for Teenagers and Their Friends.* New York: Fireside, 2000.

Matsakis, Aphrodite. *I Can't Get over It: A Handbook for Trauma Survivors.* Oakland, Calif.: New Harbinger Publications, 1996.

Williams, Mary Beth, and Soili Poijula. *The PTSD Workbook: Simple, Effective Techniques for Overcoming Traumatic Stress Symptoms.* Oakland, Calif.: New Harbinger Publications, 2002.

RELAXATION TECHNIQUES

Covey, Sean. *Daily Reflections for Highly Effective Teens.* New York: Fireside, 1999.

Davis, Martha, Matthew McKay, and Elizabeth Robbins Eshelman. *The Relaxation and Stress Reduction Workbook.* Oakland, Calif.: New Harbinger Publications, 2000.

Elkin, Allen. *Stress Management for Dummies.* Foster City, Calif.: IDG Books, 1999.

Lazarus, Judith. *Stress Relief and Relaxation Techniques.* New York: McGraw Hill, 2000.

Lite, Lori. *A Boy and a Bear: The Children's Relaxation Book.* North Branch, Minn.: Specialty Press, 1996.

Rubin, Manning. *Ways to Relieve Stress in 60 Seconds.* New York: Workman Publishing, 1993.

Wilson, Paul. *Instant Calm: Over 100 Easy-to-Use Techniques for Relaxing Mind and Body.* New York: Plume, 1995.

SELF-INJURY

Brozek, Joi. *Sleeveless.* Los Angeles: Phony Lid Publications, 2002.

Leatham, Victoria. *Bloodletting: A Memoir of Secrets, Self-Harm and Survival.* New South Wales, Australia: Allen & Unwin, 2005.

Levenkron, Steven. *Cutting: Understanding and Overcoming Self-Mutilation.* New York: W. W. Norton, 1999.

Redheffer, Judy. *Beyond the Razor's Edge: Journey of Healing and Hope beyond Self Injury.* Online: iUniverse, 2005.

Sutton, Jan. *Because I Hurt: Understanding Self Injury And Healing The Hurt.* New York: How to Books, 2006.

———. *Healing the Hurt Within: Understand Self-Injury and Self-Harm, and Heal the Emotional Wounds.* New York: How to Books, 2005.

Truner, V. J. *Secret Scars: Uncovering and Understanding the Addiction of Self-Injury.* Twin Cities, Minn.: Hazelden, 2002.

Winkler, Kathleen. *Cutting and Self-Mutilation: When Teens Injure Themselves.* Berkeley Heights, N.J.: Enslow, 2003.

SUICIDE

Crook, Marion. *Out of the Darkness: Teens Talk about Suicide.* Vancouver, British Columbia: Arsenal Pulp Press, 2004.

Esherick, Joan. *The Silent Cry: A Teen's Guide to Escaping Self-Injury and Suicide.* Broommall, Pa.: Mason Crest Publishing, 2004.

Fitzgerald, Helen. *The Grieving Teen: A Guide for Teenagers and Their Friends.* New York: Fireside, 2000.

Gootman, Marilyn E. *When a Friend Dies: A Book for Teens about Grieving and Healing.* Minneapolis: Free Spirit Publishing, 1994.

Grollman, Earl A. *Living When a Young Friend Commits Suicide, or Even Starts Talking about It.* Boston: Beacon Press, 1999.

————. *Straight Talk about Death for Teenagers: How to Cope with Losing Someone You Love.* Boston: Beacon Press, 1993.

Linn-Gust, Michelle. *Do They Have Bad Days in Heaven? Surviving the Suicide Loss of a Sibling.* Albuquerque, N.Mex.: Chellehead Works, 2001.

Nelson, Richard E., and Judith C. Galas. *The Power to Prevent Suicide: A Guide for Teens Helping Teens.* Minneapolis: Free Spirit Publishing, 1994.

Sperekas, Nicole B. *Suicide Wise: Taking Steps against Teen Suicide.* Berkeley Heights, N.J.: Enslow Publishers, 2000.

Williams, J. Mark. *Cry of Pain: Understanding Suicide and Self-Harm.* New York: Penguin, 1998.

TREATMENT

Beck, Judith S. *Cognitive Therapy: Basics and Beyond.* New York: Guilford Press, 1995.

Carter, Rosalynn. *Helping Someone with Mental Illness: A Compassionate Guide for Family, Friends, and Caregivers.* New York: Crown, 1998.

Christophersen, Edward R., and Susan L. Mortweet. *Treatments That Work with Children: Empirically Supported Strategies for Managing Childhood Problems.* Washington, D.C.: American Psychological Association, 2001.

Conterio, Karen. *Bodily Harm: The Breakthrough Healing Program for Self-Injurers.* New York: Hyperion, 1999.

Copeland, Mary Ellen, and Stuart Copans. *Recovering from Depression: A Workbook for Teens.* Baltimore: Brookes Publishing Company, 2002.

Empfield, Maureen, and Nick Bakalar. *Understanding Teenage Depression: A Guide to Diagnosis, Treatment, and Management.* New York: Owl Books, 2001.

Fassler, David G. *Help Me, I'm Sad: Recognizing, Treating, and Preventing Childhood and Adolescent Depression.* New York: Penguin Books, 1998.

Gardner, James, and Arthur H. Bell. *Overcoming Anxiety, Panic, and Depression: New Ways to Regain Your Confidence.* Franklin Lake, N.J.: Career Press, 2000.

Greenberger, Dennis. *Mind over Mood: Change How You Feel by Changing the Way You Think.* New York: Guilford Press, 1995.

Harris, Scott. *When Growing Up Hurts Too Much: A Parent's Guide to Knowing When and How to Choose a Therapist with Your Teenager.* Lanham, Md.: Taylor Trade Publishing, 2005.

Hibbs, Euthymia D., and Peter S. Jensen. *Psychosocial Treatments for Child and Adolescent Disorders: Empirically Based Strategies for Clinical Practice.* 2nd ed. Washington, D.C.: American Psychological Association, 1996.

Hipp, Earl. *Fighting Invisible Tigers: A Stress Management Guide for Teens.* Minneapolis: Free Spirit Publishing, 1995.

Kennerley, Helen. *Overcoming Anxiety: A Self-Help Guide Using Cognitive Behavioral Techniques.* New York: New York University Press, 1997.

Koplewicz, Harold S. *More Than Moody: Recognizing and Treating Adolescent Depression.* New York: Perigee Books, 2003.

Luciani, Joseph J. *Self-Coaching: How to Heal Anxiety and Depression.* New York: Wiley, 2001.

Lynn, George. *Survival Strategies for Parenting Children with Bipolar Disorder: Innovative Parenting and Counseling Techniques for Helping Children with Bipolar Disorder and the Conditions That May Occur with It.* London: Jessica Kingsley Publishing, 2000.

Pledge, Deanna S. *When Something Feels Wrong: A Survival Guide about Abuse for Young People.* Minneapolis: Free Spirit Publishing, 2002.

Schmitz, Connie C. *A Leader's Guide to Fighting Invisible Tigers: A Stress Management Guide for Teens: 12 Sessions on Stress Management and Lifeskills Development.* Minneapolis: Free Spirit Publishing, 1995.

Seaward, Brian, and Linda Bartlett. *Hot Stones and Funny Bones: Teens Helping Teens Cope with Stress and Anger.* Deerfield Beach, Fla.: Health Communications, 2002.

Sluke, Sara Jane, and Vanessa Torres. *The Complete Idiot's Guide to Dealing with Stress for Teens.* Indianapolis, Ind.: Alpha, 2001.

Waltz, Mitzi. *Bipolar Disorders: A Guide to Helping Children and Adolescents.* Sebastopol, Calif.: Patient Centered Guides, 2000.

INDEX